Living as Healer

Living as Healer

(Everyone Does Therapy and Should ... Know How)

Denton L. Roberts
with
Caddy Roberts-Williams

Hope Publishing House
Pasadena, California

For information address:

Hope Publishing House
P.O. Box 60008
Pasadena, CA 91116 - U.S.A.
Tel: (626) 792-6123 / Fax: (626) 792-2121
E-mail: hopepub@loop.com
Web site: http://www.hope-pub.com

Cover design — Michael McClary/The Workshop

Printed in the U.S.A. on acid-free paper

Library of Congress Cataloging-in-Publication Data

Roberts, Denton L.
Living as healer : everyone does therapy and should ... know how / by Denton L. Roberts, with Caddy Roberts-Williams.
p. cm.
ISBN 0-932727-96-4
1. Healing. 2. Healers. 3. Counseling. 4. Psychotherapy. I. Roberts-Williams, Caddy. II. Title.

RC480.5 .R5693 2001
158'.3--dc21 2001022281
CIP

Dedicated

to the memory of
Geraldine Gennelle Hill Roberts
1937 – 1984

"A Reliable Friend to All"

Lorna Johnston
The Change Institute

---

202 40 Ave S.W.
Calgary, AB, T2S 0X3
243-4208 287-9087

Acknowledgement:

We are deeply indebted to Robert D. Phillip, MD whose seminal work, *The Recovery of the True Self,* inspired much of the theory behind this book. We take full responsibility for the application and interpretation of Dr. Phillip's ideas.

Table of Contents

Dear Reader,

The desire to live as healer within means different things to different people. It may be that you want to be a better friend – or that you are sought out by others because you are a good listener, a valued counselor or an esteemed confidante and you want to be more effective. Perhaps you are inundated with requests for your time and attention and are looking for ways to ensure you're not creating dependencies. Maybe you are looking for better ways to take care of yourself so you don't become cynical or burn out.

In writing this book we have spent a lot of time thinking about who you are, what we have in common and what we have learned about releasing our healing power. Our intuition tells us if you picked this book up, you already know you have some capacity to be a healer – though you may not label yourself a healer. We have written the text to give you a practical guide for releasing your healing power.

We assume that you use your healing power regularly as you talk with and give counsel to your friends and colleagues and you are a person others turn to for help. We assume, you picked up this book because you not only intuitively realize that you have healing power, but you are also aware that using your power is an awesome responsibility.

Through the years we've come to recognize ourselves as healers. For both of us it has taken some time and experience to realize this. We, like you, were not informed that we had healing power in our formal and informal education. We've had to learn on our own ways to be healing. We the writers are uncle and niece. Caddy is 33 years old, and throughout her life has been someone to whom others instantly turn for help. She values being helpful to her friends, but often feels the need for guidance in order to know how far to go, what to do and how to recognize the right and wrong things to do. She is constantly looking for new ways to be a reliable and helpful friend as she relates to those who turn to her for counsel. Denton is 60 years old and has had 35 years of experience as a therapist – and has spent his adult life training ordinary people in the use of their healing power.

Through the years, Caddy and Denton have regularly discussed the *process* of counseling. Out of these ongoing conversations the idea of this book was born. From an early age both of us have been the kind of people others turn to for help with their problems. We don't know whether this has happened because of our particular nature, or whether it is just a coincidence. What we do know is, when we have been truly helpful, we ourselves have felt most fulfilled.

This is a book about the healing power of relationships. On the following pages, we blend our knowledge of the wisdom of psychotherapy with the natural caring and connection that exists in ordinary relationships. This combination is not new. The word psychotherapy literally means *soul-healing.* It is based on the natural caring and exchange of information and energy in positive, nourishing ways.

For the sake of clarity, we have written this in the first person singular, but the ideas it contains are the result of ongoing collaboration. On these pages you will find the essence of what we have discovered about releasing our healing power. We describe what we have learned in common ordinary language and use real life illustrations. What we've spelled out are tried-and-true formulas which will provide you guidance, give you confidence and help you feel safe as you exchange information and solve problems with your friends.

Introduction

Relationships have no time.
–*Charlie Rose*

Recently I received a letter from a famous artist who had visited me as a counselor more than 20 years ago. In the letter he said I had "saved his life." Since the times of our meeting, his works have been collected by major museums around the world. His art has inspired vast numbers of people and will continue to do so through the centuries. What we had done together, long ago, was simply to talk. That's all–talk.

As a result of that talking, he had abandoned some self-destructive ideas and worked through a "painter's block." Had we not talked he may have become locked in despair and confusion, or he might have talked to someone else. I do not know. I do know this: because he and I were very intentional as we talked, the relationship we developed allowed him to express his gifts more fully.

Two Basic Facts about Relationships

Fact One: Relationships last forever. This fact is mind-boggling because it means that what we do and say to one another has the most far-reaching ramifications of anything we do in life. As the writers of the Bible recognized, "The sins of the fathers are visited to the second and third generation," so we need to be aware the opposite is also true: nourishing relationships and healing acts last just as long – and will visit generations to come.

Fact Two: Relationships are the one healing power over which we have the most control. The fact that relationships represent the single healing influence we have most control over is little-recognized and under-appreciated. To the extent that we are *un*aware of the healing potential of relationships, we limit one of our greatest potentials for living helpful and meaningful lives. As we learn to be intentional about our talking, we live as healer and release the healing power within us. As we talk, sometimes we will be *those who provide* the healing. Sometimes we will be *those who receive* the healing. Often we will be both.

Recently I read in the *Dallas Morning News* the story of an African-American school teacher who was retiring after 40 years as an exemplary teacher. Her early life story was awash in tragedy for her father had killed her mother when she was very young and he was sent to prison. The six brothers and sisters landed in to various orphanages, never to see each other during their growing-up years.

In spite of all this adversity, she had managed to go through college, receive a master's degree, have a family and be an extremely productive person in society. By all outward signs, she shouldn't have succeeded. When asked about her success she said, "Although our people were not ones to believe in therapy, and I have never been to a therapist in my life, I have found that there was always the *right person* with the *right word* at the *right time.* I credit my success to those people."

So it is when someone *turns to us* for healing; they are searching for the *right word* at the *right time.* It's important to realize that *we* are their best resource, and then give them the support and counsel we have available at the time.

Talking is a Spiritual Experience

"Beneath the rock is the word," as Norman MacClean wrote in *A River Runs Through It.*

"Beneath the world is the word," as St. John said.

Talking and talking and talking, all the day long and into our dreams, daytime and nighttime, it does not cease. And maybe it can't, because, *talking is to the spirit as breathing is to the body.* As we talk, we connect at the deepest level – "deep calleth to deep", as the Psalmist says.

In some ways, we are attempting the impossible – eliciting the Spirit of the Eternal through human expression. A preposterous project! But this is the essence of being human. Maybe our talking, all of our talking – the colloquialisms, poetry, small talk, grand orations, chit-chat, musings, rapping, sermonizing, jokes and grocery list requests – is all the stuff of our lives. Maybe the all of our talking, is the closest we can ever approach being who we truly are.

Talk Therapy

The idea of talk therapy is not universally embraced by the general population – although it is something we naturally provide each other anytime we "lend an ear" and discuss life problems. Even though it is the most common form of support we instinctively give one another, as a professional skill it is still somewhat suspect within our culture. While talking through our problems is a standard healing process used from birth to death, when *talk* becomes formalized, our general culture is biased against it.

Lucille, a friend of many years, told me she went to see a psychiatrist after she had spent four years in protracted grief after her husband Charlie's untimely death. Later when she shared with her sister what she had discussed with the psychiatrist, her sister responded in a condescending tone, "Well, you sure know how to waste Charlie's money!"

Although few people find suspect the idea of seeking medical, physical or even massage therapy for bodies, the idea of using therapeutic talking exchanges to untangle or unblock thinking, is suspect in the thoughts of many. Yet, talk therapy is our most natural and common activity when life becomes difficult.

Phone calls to discuss a situation, arranging lunches with friends to talk about problems, seeking consultants on how to deal with a child or mate, and reading and discussing self-help books are just a few of many forms of talk therapy. In these activities, if we get what we need, our quandaries are clarified and we are free to go on with life. If we don't get what we need, like an untreated wound, our predicament lingers, festers and may distort every aspect of our life.

My friend Tom tells this story about growing up. He was the last of six children, a big and clumsy toddler. When it came time for him to learn to tie his shoes, his mother found he did not readily catch on. Since she was overloaded with responsibilities and could think of no way to teach him this skill, she gave up and taught him an improvised way. Now a man of 60, Tom has never learned to tie a bow knot. He is an intelligent, capable person, a good friend and devoted father; unfortunately, this early experience still affects his self-concept, for he still occasionally mentions what a slow learner he is and then goes on to validate this conclusion by pointing out, "I can't even tie my shoes."

Such examples show how unsolved situations have lasting repercussions. Failure to solve the seemingly simple task of learning to tie his shoes has affected Tom's whole life. While this may seem like a minor issue, many such trivial issues can prove equally limiting in terms of a person's self-concept. So, our failures at solving even the simplest of problems may affect our whole life.

Beginning

As you start this book, we recommend you pause and recall a few of the persons who have most positively influenced your life. The exercise at the end of this chapter will help you understand the importance of this. As you remember these individuals, think about what they have in common. In doing this you will begin to recognize that it is the people you admire most, living and dead, who have succeeded in releasing their healing power with you.

From the great spiritual leaders to the framers of the Constitution – from outstanding humanitarians to humble servants – from Nobel Peace Prize winners to the persons next door – the people most admired, are those who successfully release their healing power. Whether their efforts are directed toward world order, caring for the dispossessed of society or simply being a good friend, they are people who provide – the *right word* at the *right time*.

What we are highlighting as we write about releasing the healer within are the impulses and urges that cause one person to reach out to another. It is the part of you that is willing, even eager, to be helpful to someone else and that longs for meaningful companionship. It is the part of you that works for peace and harmony in relationships, families, communities and in the world and that drives you to compassionate action. It feels pain when you witness another's suffering and adversity. And, ultimately this part of you intuitively knows that you somehow have the power to "help make the wounded whole."

Through meaningful communication the *one* healing power over which we have full control is exercised. In the final analysis, this book is an outline which describes how to be effective as a *reliable friend*. Technically, it is about the *power* of talk-therapy. However, it is talk-therapy in the broadest sense. *Talk,* as we are using it, means having meaningful communication exchanges, and *therapy* means exercising healing power.

It is through meaningful communication exchanges,

verbal and nonverbal, that we establish nurturing and nourishing friendships, build strong families, create stable societies and pursue happiness. In the human family there's no question of whether or not you will be called on to exert healing power. You will. The only question is will you be equipped to be effective when called upon?

Professional Persons

Most of us have felt the warm glow that comes when we realize we have been truly helpful with a friend. Likewise, we have felt the stress we experience when we have failed to find a way to be helpful to someone we care about who is in need. A professional is someone who has mastered a skill or body of information. As persons, we all qualify for professional status. Since, *we are all professional persons*–the better we know *what to do* and *when to do it*–as we interact with each other, the more useful we will be to one another and ultimately the more fulfilled we be.

Healing and Wounding

On the following pages we use the *healer/wounded* metaphor to describe the nature of meaningful human exchanges. While at first this metaphor appears to be a little strong, we think it best describes how we give and receive caring. There are two factors in life that guarantee we will be wounded and need healing. The first is *free will*, which is inside us. The second is *environmental-reality*, which is outside of us.

Free will and environmental realities are both a blessing and a curse. As a blessing, free will is the power we have to shape our lives into something meaningful. As a blessing, environmental realities are the nourishing, life-giving relationships we have with others and nature. As a curse, free will allows us to override or modify our instinct and venture beyond our capacities. As a curse, environmental realities are simply the honest recognitions that there are situations that are toxic to human well- being.

Since we possess free will, we inevitably overreach – get out on a limb – and into situations that we don't have the skill, background, experience or ability to negotiate. Thus free will causes us to end up wounded from time to time. On the other hand, since society, even nature, provides environments that are unhealthy, we suffer wounding regularly from conditions not of our making.

An example of how free will wounding occurs is seen in the common experiences we label as failures. Bill, a competent, well-educated adult, took on the responsibility of being the foster-parent for two emotionally disturbed teenagers. Before long his life was in a shambles. He found he couldn't communicate adequately with these young men, and ultimately they ended up being arrested and placed in the juvenile justice system.

Bill felt like a failure. However, even though he had failed with the young men, he was not *a failure.* He cared about them and had done his best. He was still a competent adult. Yet he thought of himself as a failure because he had overreached his skill and ability by taking on a responsibility he wasn't equipped to handle.

Kiama was in her 70s, a Japanese/American grandmother. In her latter years she became depressed as she realized that throughout her adult life she had regarded herself as a second-class citizen and feared she'd passed on that same inaccurate self-assessment to her children and grandchildren. In therapy, as she traced the idea of being a second-class citizen to its origins, she realized it began when her family was sent to an interment camp during World War II. Her wounding was a result of an environmental reality – one over which she had no control.

We all have wounds as a result of exercising free will and experiencing environmental reality. Wounding in life is inescapable, but we also possess the power to heal and be healed. This power is characterized by our ability to establish healthy relations (interdependent relationships) and talk through the troubling realities of our lives. Healthy interdependent relationships are those in which we share our information, knowledge, experience and pain – intellectually and emotionally.

Bill and Kiama each sought me out for help. Thankfully, I'd learned enough about releasing healing power to help them put their lives back in right order. Once the wounds of free will were healed, Bill stopped thinking of himself as a failure and moved on with his life, somewhat wiser for the experience. Once the wounds of her environmental reality were healed, Kiama no longer saw herself as a second-class citizen and was free to give her unique gifts to her children and grandchildren.

Another paradoxical factor important to bear in mind in this regard is that since wounding and healing is inevitable throughout life, they are also a major growth processes – *Tis an ill-wind that does not blow some good.* Fortunately, each successful act of healing leaves both the wounded and the healer stronger than before.

In scientific circles the saying goes: "Good judgment comes from experience and experience comes from bad judgment." With some modification this truism applies to the naturel wounding-healing sequence. Our ability to be healers comes from having experienced healing ourselves; our needs for healing are the result of having been wounded. By virtue of our humanness we will be wounded and by the same virtue we have the power to be healers.

Our healing power is exercised primarily through *intentional* talking. Not all talking is intentional. Most of our talking can best be described as incidental – the result of an incident or coincidence. However, occasionally we are very intentional as we talk – we talk to solve problems. When our talk becomes intentional (problem-solving) we are seeking and/or providing therapy – healing. We are communicating in order to resolve a life issue – to heal a wound. When talk becomes intentional, knowing what to do and how to do it is critical.

Through intentional communication we are invaluable resources to one another. Whenever our talking becomes intentional, we establish a wounded/healer dialogue either consciously or unconsciously. Through intentional talking we bond and establish relationships that are interdependent – we experience caring on a deep level. Through intentional talking we experience intimacy.

To live as healer, it is essential to know as much as we can about how to develop and maintain healing dialogues.

Exercise

Completing this exercise will help you to recognize how intentional talk has positively effected your life thus far.

1. List the ten persons who have had the greatest positive influences in your life. These can either be people you've known or historical role-models.

2. Contemplate the list and note five or ten characteristics each of these people have in common.

3. Reflect on how these characteristics have had healing influences in your life.

4. Write a short one-page essay on their importance to you.

1

Releasing Your Healer

Some years ago I attended a training workshop with Robert L. Goulding, MD, the psychiatrist who developed the internationally esteemed Redecision Therapy. Observing him work with clients to resolve old festering self-limiting problems, I and the others in the group were inspired by his clinical skills and were in awe of his ability to get to the heart of a matter quickly, yet with care and compassion. We were impressed as we experienced the healing power of intentional talk.

A few days into the training, one of the participants approached Dr. Goulding at a break and announced so all could hear, "I just wanted to let you know, Dr. Goulding, that I am going to be a better therapist than you."

Those of us who overheard the conversation thought "fat chance." This particular individual had been a rather unlikable sort and had done nothing in the sessions to demonstrate he had much therapeutic skill or sensitivity. We waited for Goulding's response.

After a brief pause he said, "I certainly hope so. I am giving you the accumulated knowledge I've gained in 35 years experience – if you're not a better therapist than I, I'll have failed *my* objectives."

It is in this spirit that we write this book.

What Is Therapy?

Therapy in the broadest sense of the word means healing power. We apply therapy when we clean a wound or put on a Band-Aid or when we bring chicken soup to a friend with a cold. Therapy is best understood as the power we possess to help one another heal – physically and psychologically.

Throughout life most of us *have been* methodically taught how to assist ourselves and one another in wound healing and in giving supportive nurturing at times of illness. Yet, we *have not been* methodically taught how to use the power of talk to heal psychic wounds. On the pages that follow we are using therapy to refer to psychic healing *generally*, and the healing that occurs when we really talk to one another *specifically*. Before we can effectively and comfortably use our healing power, we have to be able to answer questions like the following:

- How do I know when I am really being helpful?
- How do I keep from taking on people's problems?
- How do I let people know it's okay to open up?
- How can I know that I am not doing harm?

These are the questions we are addressing as we write.

A skilled surgeon uses a scalpel and makes precise interventions. Eric Berne, MD, the father of Transactional Analysis, states: "Doing psychotherapy is like practicing surgery" and "you don't want someone doing surgery randomly, with a butcher knife."

This admonition is equally true for releasing your healing power through meaningful talk. In order to live as healer effectively, you need to know what is helpful, what is harmful and how to make useful interventions.

Through the years we have been motivated by our situations, inclinations and problems to develop our skills as professional healers. Along the way, we have worked with a broad variety of clients ranging from prison inmates to Hollywood celebrities, in a variety of settings from free clinics and drug abuse programs to Beverly Hills private offices – both in formal settings because of our professional positions and informally in self-help groups. Most of all we have worked with each other, our family and friends, in informal problem-solving.

As students we have studied old and new therapies, attended workshops and training in innovative and traditional therapies. Like so many, had we known years ago what we know now, we would have saved ourselves and others precious time and needless suffering.

Which brings us to the question: What would we have liked to have had in hand as we started this journey?

Our conclusion has been that what we would have liked was something that would have helped *demystify* the therapy process while providing us a safe process to follow–*a handbook of what to do and what not to do.* We agreed, it would have been most beneficial if we had had something we could have used personally as a guide, as well as pass on to the people who sought our assistance. Such a resource would have let us know where to begin and helped us understand what we were about–giving us an order with which to proceed.

So we decided to provide what would have been helpful for us–a book to provide healers with directions that allow them to safely, effectively and consciously release the power of their caring, and a book healers can share with those who are seeking their counsel.

Acknowledging That We Are Healers

A first step is to begin thinking of yourself as a healer –because it helps you understand the true nature of requests for help that you receive day-by-day. The more we think of ourselves as healers, the more effective we will be with each other as we deal with the give-and-take of life. Besides, we will be better friends, parents and members of society when we *all* perceive of ourselves as sources for healing with one another.

It might feel pretentious to label yourself a healer, but it is humbling, as well as gratifying, to realize that you have healing power. In fact, you begin the process of releasing the healer within by recognizing that *any* request for your counsel is based upon someone's intuitive recognition that you are their best resource for help.

Naturally we tend to be unsure of ourselves when we receive requests to enter another person's dilemma. Years ago, I consulted my mentor when asked to provide counseling in a situation where I was very hesitant to proceed. After hearing my concerns he said, "The person someone turns to in time of need is the person most likely to be helpful – even when your helpfulness is simply making an informed caring referral to a competent professional."

Through the years, I have found this to be sage advice. My mentor helped me realize that a request for my help is based on the intuitive recognition that I was the person's best resource.

By thinking of yourself as a healer and by recognizing requests for your healing power, you begin to understand both the *true honor* and the *awesome responsibility* such requests entail.

Recently at a TOPS (Take Off Pounds Sensibly) meeting, Susie, one of the members, was very disappointed with her weekly weigh-in. With a nervous laugh she asked the leader, Sharon, how she could keep from eating a whole box of cookies. Sharon then had a choice. She could come back with a quick TOPS standard reply like, "Don't keep any cookies in the house," or she could see herself as the healer she is. Sharon took Susie's request seriously and reached out to her and said, "I know how you feel." She arranged to sit down privately with Susie so they could talk about Susie's feelings of being out of control and the disappointment of the weight gain. I n Sharon and Susie's story, you can see how we are given many seemingly superficial opportunities to act as healers. When we think of ourselves as healers, we begin to look beyond the superficial and thus have the opportunity to offer caring, compassionate counsel.

Healthy relationships offer healing. When Bob asks Jean to help him think through a problem at work, he is asking her to function as a healer. When Sue asks Patti to help her figure out what to do when her daughter has a temper tantrum, she is asking Patti to function as a healer. When Fred asks Ted for advice on how to deal with the boss, he is asking him to function as a healer. When Molly asks Paul to give her some feedback on how to get along with her father, she is asking him to act as a healer. *Anytime* we reach out to another with a problem – we are *asking* for the healing balm of caring counsel.

This normal asking and responding may not generally be thought of as a request for healing, but if we are going to tell it like it is, *asking for healing* is what it is! Each successful healing of even seemingly small-scale problems restores balance and health and precludes that these small issues become large issues sometime in the future. Had Bill and Kiama not talked about the wounding of being a failure and a second-class citizen, their whole lives could have been distorted because of their inaccurate self concepts.

Thus living as healers with one another is critical to both personal and social well-being. When we look realistically at our societal problems, a good case can be made for the fact that our prisons and our hospitals are filled with people who have not received adequate help in learning to solve their life problems. Further, it is a well-established that becoming overloaded with life problems causes psychological as well as physical difficulties. People under stress tend to "act-out" in anti-social behavior or to "act-in" in emotional and physical disorders.

Since thinking of yourself as a healer may seem pretentious at first, we do not recommend it as a *title.* Nonetheless it is important to recognize you have *healing* power so you can recognize requests for your counsel for what they are.

Review

Let's review the essential content of this chapter. There are certain premises you will need to fix in your mind for the rest of this book if it is to be useful to you.

1. Therapy is healing power.

2. We have not been adequately taught how to use our healing power.

3. Talk therapy is often thought of as suspect in our society.

4. You are being asked to be a healer when your counsel is requested.

5. Wounds left unhealed affect your self-concept.

6. It is important to think of yourself as a healer in order to begin living as healer.

2

What You Need to Know to Be Useful

There are three natural healing processes built into humans: the physical processes of *wound healing*, the *immune response* and the psychic *process* of interdependent relationships. We have little or no control over the processes of wound healing and immune responses. These processes engage automatically when we have physical wounds or are invaded by an infection or virus. With these natural healing processes all we can do is support their automatic healing actions by using antiseptics, antibiotics, good nutrition and rest.

Psychic healing, on the other hand, is the process we have the most control over for it occurs through healthy exchanges of information and nurture between people. This chapter explains how we can refine our skills to effectively use this process as a healer/reliable friend.

The First Step

The most common natural model for being a *healer/reliable-friend* is ideal parenting – which does three things:

- ✷ provides clear limits;
- ✷ provides adequate information;
- ✷ provides direct nurture.

To exercise your personal healing power following this formula for good parenting gives you a much needed guide. As a healer, it is important you have clear limits, adequate information and direct nurture. How to do this is the key.

Cries and Coos

We cry when wounded. We coo when healed. An infant has *only* cries and coos with which to communicate distress and well-being. Adults have many more ways of expressing themselves. However, their expressions of *dis-ease* and *ease* can be boiled down to sophisticated cries and coos. A call for help in whatever form is a cry. A sense of well-being however expressed is a coo. Healing in the context of cries and coos can be viewed as the process of resolving the cries and fostering the coos. Simply stated, what you need to know to be useful as a healer is how to help someone move from crying to cooing.

A simple formula we follow when talking with friends about problems consists of first, creating trust and safety; second, helping them express their feelings; third, facilitating their discovering what has caused the feelings. Finally, assisting them discover ways to resolve the situation that caused the crying.

Professionals call this process *creating therapeutic alliances*. Such alliances are technical terms for reliable-friendship. This is one we know we can turn to for support, comfort, sound advice and clear direction no matter what our condition. Being a healer is being a reliable-friend in the best sense of the word.

Natural Processes

When an infants cry, they will naturally intensify the volume until a parent or someone discovers and alleviates the source of discomfort. If nobody is available or able to detect and correct the source of discomfort, by virtue of a natural biological process, this crying eventually changes to sobbing–which is caused by a biochemical reaction within the infant's system. This reaction eventually induces sleep. When they awake, infants will repeat the cycle until such a time as the situation causing the stress is relieved.

This same natural process goes on in a variety of subtle forms with fully grown human beings. Our crying may be disguised; it can be having the *blues*, it can be *raging*, it can be *acting out*. It may take many different forms. When we are troubled, we, like the infant under the stress of unrelieved pain, will eventually become exhausted. However, once we regain our strength we repeat the sequence. This will go on and cause stress until we get relief. When we cry in pain, no matter what form that crying takes, we naturally intensify our response until we make something happen that relieves our stress.

Commonly we do something to anesthetize ourselves

artificially – like engaging in substance abuse. Unfortunately artificial solutions for easing our pain that don't lead to resolution may end up as addictions. Eric Berne in *Games People Play* states, "Alcohol and drugs are *instead* of people." What he realized was that the cries of life cannot be treated adequately through substances like drugs and alcohol, but are often turned to when we lack nurturing people in our lives. Through the years we have dealt with many teenagers and adults who have had substance-abuse problems. We have yet to encounter one of these who had adequate reliable friends with whom they could discuss their pain.

The Task of the Healer

The conditions of the womb provide a natural model for your task as a healer, as you will want to duplicate these conditions of the womb in your relationship in order to create an ideal healing environment. Generally the womb provides:

- a contained protected environment;
- being surrounded by warmth;
- connection to a reliable source of nourishment.

Comments are jokingly made about wanting to return to the womb, but we suggest that this is no joking matter. Cooing – our expressions of satisfaction – occurs when our life situation approximates the natural conditions of the womb and we feel *contained, warmed* and *nourished.*

In the womb, containment is provided by the uterine walls, warmth comes from the amniotic fluid and nourishment is given by the mother's system through the umbilical chord. These are the conditions you will need to replicate in your relationship as a healer.

Ultimately a healer seeks to help the wounded *establish* and *maintain* conditions in ordinary life that resemble these elements. A healer assists the wounded to develop necessary skills to replicate this state inside and outside the counseling context. Thus, by learning to create and arrange for support, warmth and adequate supplies of nourishment (physical and psychic) the wounded develop their own abilities to avoid future wounding and to heal themselves.

Over the years, in giving counsel to many couples, I have asked them to describe the good times, back in the "in love" days. They tell about being together in conditions that resemble the conditions of the womb – warmth, containment and nourishment. In assisting them to make the marriage work, I have often used this analogy to diagnose their situation and suggest actions they can take in the present to move beyond their difficulties and conflicts.

Feelings Are the Keys

Feelings are instant indicators, although often complex. For example, I can be writing when unexpectedly I hear a car skid to a stop on the street outside. Suddenly I feel adrenaline in my system. Alarmed, my whole body is on watch. As I turn my attention to the street, my heart rate accelerates putting me on red alert.

There is nothing, aside from tuning out the environment, I can do to avoid this natural response. Hearing the car screech naturally sends an electrical charge through my brain that relays the message to my endocrine system which begins releasing certain chemicals into my blood stream to help me summon the energy to cope with the situation. What I can do at that point is use my sense of alert to check out the danger and act appropriately. As I do this, I restore my psychological and physiological systems to their normal balance.

While we cannot stop feelings from occurring, we can and do learn what to do with them. Knowing how to cope with and resolve feelings is the key to being an effective healer. However, for many, our families and education did not teach us how to deal with feelings. To be effective as healers it is important we develop an in-depth understanding of the message of feelings, as well as the skill to help others understand the signals their feelings are sending.

In order to develop our understanding and skill, let's begin by reviewing authentic feelings and the actions that bring them to resolution.

Feelings, while complex, vary in degree and intensity. Authentic feelings can be classified under four broad categories: *anger, fear, sadness* and *joy*. Each of these have many varieties, yet although we have many names for feelings, they all may be classified under these four broad categories.

Each authentic feeling calls for a specific action in order for it to resolve. Anger calls for *redress*. Fear calls for *protection*. Sadness calls for *comfort*. Joy calls for *companionate-celebration*.

While we do not like to use technical words like *re-*

dress and *companionate-celebration,* there are times when the exact word is important. To understand these concepts, we will illustrate and define them, for they are essential if you are to be effective in healing endeavors. It is when feelings are expressed and met with an appropriate response from the healer that they begin to resolve–cries will become coos. Feelings not met with appropriate responses will linger or escalate. Thus unresolved anger ultimately becomes rage, sadness becomes depression, fear becomes anxiety and joy left uncelebrated becomes mania.

The following chart illustrates this information:

Feeling	Resolving Action Called for	Left Unresolved Becomes
Anger	Redress	Rage
Sadness	Comfort	Depression
Fear	Protection	Anxiety
Joy	Companionate-Celebration	Mania

Most naturally, a wounded person turns to a healer with cries. Cries, however subtle and disguised, are expressions of pain. A healer's task is to help the wounded identify the *cause* of the wounding, the *message* of the feeling and the *action* needed to resolve the feeling–that is to heal.

The following examples illustrate how this is done in normal life.

Example One

Bill is furious with his boss and decides to call Maria

to talk about it. As Maria listens to his story she hears his anger and frustration. By listening she is beginning to help him get in touch with his authentic feeling. In this case, Bill recognizes his anger and his desire to get even.

Maria, as a healer, knows that anger comes from real or perceived abuse or exploitation. She also knows anger is a call for redress. By listening and sharing her understanding of the message of the actual feeling she helps him to understand that getting even would only escalate the situation. She helps him see what he wants is redress. Recognizing she is a healer, Maria helps him figure out what action he can take to resolve the feeling. Redress evens things up (this is what redress means). Maria listens to Bill's story and helps him see that *getting even* is different from *evening things up*. Getting even may only raise the stakes in difficult situations.

The gist of Bill's story is that his supervisor is constantly favoring one of his colleagues. In this specific instance, one of Bill's good ideas has been attributed to this colleague. As Bill talks this through, his anger subsides and Maria helps him focus on what he can do to even things up. Bill concludes he needs to bring his concerns out in the open and he and Maria make a plan he thinks will resolve the situation.

When Bill addresses the situation with his boss, his boss denies his favoritism, but Bill feels relieved because he has stated his concern and developed a plan he can use to confront future situations as they occur. Through using Maria as his healer, Bill has gained clarity about what to do when he becomes angry – a skill he can use throughout his life.

It is good to note that healing in this instance, and as is often the case, is not the result of winning or changing others. Healing occurs when we can identify the message of our feelings and effectively act in a way honors our feelings.

Example Two

Jeani calls Sue to get some advice. She is fearful to the point of near panic because she is about to commit in a new relationship and her boyfriend has asked her to get an AIDS test. While she has no reason to think she could test positive, she is frightened on several fronts: What if she did test positive? What if people found out she was going for an AIDS test? What if she tested positive and her ex-husband found out and took her children from her?

Sue, as the healer, knows the healthy resolution of fear, real or imagined, occurs when the wounded feels protected. As Sue talks to Jeani, Sue helps Jeani isolate her fear and reassures her by volunteering to get reliable information about confidential testing. The conversation ends with Jeani calmer and looking forward to her planned trip to see her boyfriend. As it turns out, Jeani is not HIV-positive and she is able to begin the relationship without undue anxiety.

Example Three

Rosie is depressed–and has been since her mother became gravely ill. Lately she has been sleeping through the day and having insomnia at night. She calls Marshall, long-time friend, and tells him she doesn't know what's wrong with her. They arrange to have lunch together. As they talk, Rosie admits feeling blue ever since she found out her mother was dying. She keeps telling herself she should be using this time to help her mother and enjoy being close to her while she's still alive, but she's just too depressed. Marshall acknowledges he can understand that and asks her what she is doing about her sadness.

Marshal knows sadness – which is not met with comfort – becomes depression. He offers to be the person she can turn to for comfort and they agree to meet and talk regularly during difficult times. Rosie's depression lightens and she feels more capable of doing what she would like to do with her mother.

Example Four

Joe receives a big promotion at work – the culmination of ten years on the corporate ladder. By nature Joe is a cool, calm, collected type, a steady company man and doesn't make a big deal of his promotion. In fact, instead of celebrating this success, he increases his work schedule, taking on more and more projects after his promotion. He becomes so hyped-up he can't sleep well because of all the ideas running through his mind.

At work he pushes himself harder and pushes his team harder as well. Although realizing he is becoming a workaholic, Joe can't relax, much less enjoy his success. Finally he calls Mack to tell him what's happening. Mack knows that the authentic feeling joy is consummated through companionate-celebration (celebrating with companions).

As he listens to Joe's story, Mack inquires about the promotion asking Joe what he has done to celebrate his success. Together they plan an appropriate festivity to pay tribute to the accomplishment of ten years of hard work. Joe's mania subsides and he begins to enjoy his new position without making outrageous demands of himself and others.

These four vignettes illustrate the importance of having an informed healer available as we go through the up-and-downs of life. Any of these situations – Bill's anger, Jeani's fear, Rosie's sadness, or Joe's joy – left without the healing embrace of a reliable-friend could potentially lead to serious personal difficulties. Recognizing the cries of life as cries, and working with wounded friends to help them coo, even in the most ordinary and casual situations, is the work of a healer. Such work, when done well, can alleviate much suffering.

A Word of Caution

It's important to recognize that just because you have healing powers does not mean you are adequate to all cries for help. Nor that you will always have enough surplus energy to meet every need you encounter. As a healer it's essential to be aware of your limits in order not to overtax or overburden yourself. Equally, it is important to know you can often be a healer/reliable-friend when you merely express your concern and support and advise someone to seek professional help.

The better you are at accurately assessing and clearly stating your limits, the more effective healer you will be.

If your situation is such so that you can only comfortably spare 30 minutes to discuss a problem with someone, let them know your limits. They will be better able to understand when you need to stop, and they won't feel they imposed on you.

One day my son called when he was in a midst of a serious romance. He and his girl friend were having communication difficulty. After hearing him out a bit, I told him I did not feel I was his best resource on that particular topic and recommended a couple of persons he could talk to. As time went by, I checked up on him to see how things were going. That was several years ago. Recently he asked if I remembered that conversation. Frankly, I didn't until he jogged my memory. "I just wanted to tell you," he said, "you were really helpful. Not only did I get the help I needed, but I also learned it was enough for me to give my friends a referral when I didn't feel adequate to handle their requests."

By acknowledging our limits and honestly expressing them in a supportive way, we are practicing a form of healing, for we are *modeling*. Modeling is demonstrating good self-care by the way we handle our own life. Some sage has said, "If we don't respect our own limits we will either *burn-out, drop-out, opt-out* or *flip-out.*"

We all set limits either directly or indirectly – either explicitly or implicitly. An effective healer sets limits directly and explicitly. So if you should have a friend who is suicidal and feel you don't have the expertise to deal with this, you would naturally stay with your friend until you got a competent professional came on the scene. That would be the healing thing to do; within your limits.

Failure to recognize your limits in such a situation could end up disastrously for you both. Knowing and setting your limits in less critical situations also avoids disaster.

Important Points to Remember from this Chapter

1. Cries and coos are natural expressions that express the need of a healer.

2. There are four basic emotions that call for specific acts of healing:
   * Anger calls for redress
   * Fear calls for protection
   * Sadness calls for comfort
   * Joy calls for companionate-celebration

3. Knowing your limits is critical to being an effective healer.

4. Referral to a competent professional is a healing act.

3

Listening is Healing

Lee Iacocca, retired president of Chrysler corporation, has stated that what he looks for in leadership is a good listener. There is hardly anything more supportive than being listened to. When we feel someone is really listening we feel connected on the deepest level. In those times when we feel listened to, our separateness is transcended and we become one with another for a time (we experience a time of intimacy).

In fact both the listener and the speaker benefit when true communication takes place. The speaker gets the experience of being truly heard and the listener is afforded a chance to experience the reality of another. An important truism is "the quality of the dialogue determines the quality of the relationship."

Interestingly, we find that the better we are at listening, the less we feel the need to intervene; consequently, the more effective our interventions become. In healing dialogues, listening allows us to make an empathic connection with the person's joy, pain or difficulty. Experiencing an empathic connection is often all people need to find their own resources for solving problems. On innumerable occasions throughout our careers when we did not know what to do except listen, we have had these encounters end with a genuine thank-you. We often wonder what we have done to deserve the thank-you, but now we know – what we did was listen.

The better we become at listening the more potent healers we become. This is due in part to the fact that when we truly listen we forsake our own considerations and lend our full attention to the other. As this occurs the person with the problem feels supported and is able to draw more fully on their own internal resources. Partly this is because when we truly listen we perceive the essence of the situation and when it comes time to intervene we can do so with astute accuracy.

Bill, a middle-aged manager in a social service agency, called and asked if I had time to talk. I agreed and he told me his situation at work as well as with his wife and children was becoming unbearable. I then heard a long dissertation from him how everyone expected him to be able to solve what he perceived to be unsolvable problems.

In Bill's view, much of his difficulties stemmed from being raised by a passive mother and an alcoholic father. "They always made me feel responsible for their problems, just like my boss, wife and kids are doing now." He then described a childhood that anyone would agree should have never happened to anyone.

After listening for a long time to his detailed description, I finally asked if his wife, boss and children knew of his feelings. "No," he said, "they're too caught up in their own stuff to care about what's going on with me."

"That seems very similar to the situation you described with your parents," I said.

"Exactly," he said.

After a long pause, I finally asked, "Would you be comfortable asking them whether or not they cared about what's going on with you?"

"Well, I could ask, but it won't do any good," he replied.

"That's all I can think of," I told him. "Why not do it and let me know what happens?"

He did. A few days later he called to say that after their initial curiosity about why he raised such a foolish question, he had a meaningful conversation with each of them.

Bill had taken an important first step in resolving conflict within his immediate family and with his supervisor at work. By communicating openly and honestly with them, he opened the door for a more fulfilling relationship with each of them.

Yet he was wise enough to know this was only a beginning and there was more work to do. "My problem with them is not solved, but I feel better," he said. Bill's sense of *feeling better*, no doubt came from a new found sense of empowerment.

Had I not listened to Bill's problem or simply offered him some *quick* analysis or solution, I doubt he would have done much more than recite an old familiar story. However, since I chose to be a reliable-friend and listen until he told the whole story, as well as honestly acknowledge I could only offer the suggestion for him to tell them how he felt, we came to a potentially healing solution. Telling those connected to us what we are feeling, is the natural way to living as healer. In this case, Bill only needed help to see this as part of the problem-solving process.

Later Bill told me that he applied this process – telling others what he was feeling – in several difficult arenas of his life. His first success led to more of the same, not only with his family and supervisor, but expanding into his circle of friends and co-workers, as well. As general rule, one successful healing almost always leads to more success.

Five Phenomena of Listening

As you listen to someone's story, one or more of the following will likely happen: You will be intrigued, bored, lost, insightful or – in technical terms – in parallel-process. All are mostly self-explanatory, except perhaps the last. *Intrigued* – you will be fascinated by the unfolding drama. *Bored* – you will find the story uninteresting and irrelevant. *Lost* – you will be confused by the story and not know how the pieces fit together. *Insightful* – you will see into the situation and make significant connection between the story you are hearing and the situation that brings you together. *Parallel-process* – you will be identifying the commonality/parallels between the person's situation and your own life situation. Each of these listening phenomena is important to the healer and to the wounded. Each holds its special meaning.

A psychiatrist I know tells the story of dozing off while a client was telling her story. When she noticed that he had fallen asleep she was angry and stood up and kicked him in the shins. He was embarrassed, apologetic and pained by the situation. As time went on, they analyzed what happened and found that what had gone on between them was amazingly similar to situations that brought her to go into therapy in the first place. As it was, she felt that people weren't listening to her and that what she thought and felt didn't count. They found by carefully analyzing both the story she was telling and what went on between them they were able to get to the essence of her dilemma.

Both the stories being told and the dynamics between the wounded and the healer are important elements in the healing process. Thus it is vital to reflect on the five phenomena of listening to see how they inform the healing process.

Intriguing

The most compelling stories you hear as a healer are stories that are intriguing because they are fresh and dynamic. For the healer such stories can also be seductive. Sometimes you'll get so caught up in the drama you forget why the story is being told. With intriguing stories, you need to remind yourself constantly that the issue is to get to the nature of the wounding and you will have to keep asking yourself, "What does this have to do with the problem presented?"

Arnie, a master of good storytelling, regaled the therapist and the group with tales from his past. In most of these he was the hero – able to put others in their place while being a rather cocky character. His stories were engaging and he came off as a precocious young man. If I, as the healer, simply got caught up in the story and did not listen to the process the stories had in common, I would be greatly entertained but would miss the point of what these stories had to do with his seeking counsel, because if he was such a hero, why was he here? It turned out his wife had told him she would leave him if he put her down one more time.

Usually, those telling the stories are able to make the connection between the story and what's going on in their lives. Sometimes it might take a little coaxing like – "I'm sure this story has some relevance to your current dilemma. Let's figure out what it is."

Arnie eventually came to see his stories were a way to bolster his ego, but this ploy was no longer working with his wife. As soon as he told his wife about his insight in counseling, they made an agreement that she should confront him whenever he fell into the familiar pattern. They began to work together to figure out what he was *truly* needing to feel better about himself.

I had learned, long before Arnie came along, that when people introduce what seems to be extraneous information into the clinical setting, it usually had a connection to what was bringing them into treatment. I had also learned that when the connection between the seemingly extraneous story and the person's reason for being in therapy was obscured, it was the time to ask "What does this story have to do with your reason for being here?"

With intriguing stories it is important to give primary attention to process (how one thing leads to another) and secondary attention to content (what this story is about). This discipline once developed allows you as the healer to cut to the chase in many complicated situations. A therapist needs always to be asking the question: " What's going on here?" According to Eric Berne this question keeps you focused on process – how things fit together – as you listen to intriguing stories.

Bored

A second phenomenon of listening is being bored. Tales that have been told over and over are usually tiresome. Fred, a chronic complainer, goes on at great length about how his wife Julie misunderstands him – telling the story of their conflict in a whinny, won't-you-feel-sorry-for-me? voice.

Listening to such you find your mind wandering and you wishing the storyteller would knock it off and get on with life. Then you begin to think about irrelevancies like what you'll prepare for dinner or why that man walking by the window chose to wear a flannel shirt on such a hot day. When stories are boring it's hard to intervene without implying the storyteller is a bore. While this might be an accurate observation, it is not the kind of intervention that will lead to healing.

When you find that you are weary with a story it is fair to assume that the storyteller is also bored, although not fully aware of this. A query like, "What would you rather be doing right now?" is often productive. People who tell boring stories are stuck in life, and the task of the healer is to help them get out of the rut they are in.

Confusing

Some stories are confusing. You get lost in the content. As a healer, if you try to make sense of the story you often get inundated in a quagmire of irrelevancy. Just as you can't give a clear answer to a foggy question, you can't get a clear picture from a muddled story.

Here, too, the best strategy for the healer is to ask the person what this story has to do with their current problem. It is fair to assume that if you find yourself lost in a morass of detail and seemingly irrelevant facts, the person telling the story is just as befuddled and trying to find how the pieces of life fits together. As you focus the storyteller on the relevance of the story to the current situation, they'll often come up with the missing links and clarify the picture for both of you. When stories are confusing, your best strategy is to keep the storyteller telling you how the story applies to the situation.

Insightful

Some stories cause the lights to go on for both the teller and the listener. These are stories of insight – interesting and exciting – so the healer and the wounded feel they are getting somewhere in therapy, and they are.

These tales need to be heard. When stories are poignant with insight, it is best for the listener simply to underline and highlight insights as they pop up. Having insight is a good indicator that healing is taking place. Statements like "You are really putting the pieces together." "It seems like you are on your own side." "That is a whole new way of looking at your old problem." or "Now you're cooking," reinforce the storyteller's insight – which is a primary healing tool characterized by bringing together diverse pieces of life.

Parallel-Process

Parallel-process, as it is called in professional circles, is simply the storyteller's dilemma and the listener's life experience coming together in parallel. When this happens, a frank acknowledgment of its occurrence is generally productive. "Your situation greatly parallels my situation in life," is usually heard as a supportive statement affirming the bond between you. It helps you to stay focused on the storyteller's information and not what's going on with you.

When parallel-process occurs, the healer/listeners may experience an erosion of confidence in themselves as healers. As this happens it is common to have thoughts like, "I can't be useful to this person since I have the same things going on in my life."

This is not true. Professional counselors learn, through the years, that at times their clients deal with some of the current considerations of their own lives better than they, the counselors, are. Just because you are not doing so well in certain areas of your own life does not mean you cannot be useful.

Frequently when you experience parallel-process, you will come to some significant insights into your own situation. This is a fringe benefit of being a good listener and an affirmation that we all live some of the time in the wounded-healer paradigm.

Important Points of this Chapter

The important things to fix in your mind presented in this chapter are:

1. It's OK just to listen.

2. Listening is important—it establishes an empathic connection.

3. The dynamics of the story are as important as the content.

4. The five phenomena of listening are:
   - *intriguing*
   - *boring*
   - *lost*
   - *insightful*
   - *parallel-process*

4

Keeping Focus

Perhaps the most under-recognized power that we human beings have is the freedom of focus. Just as it is true that what you eat you become, so it is true what you focus on and consort with becomes your reality. Thus far we have been encouraging you to focus on:

- your healing power – by recognizing yourself as a healer;
- the healing function of healthy interdependent relationships; and
- listening as the access to healing.

Keeping focus for both the wounded and the healer is critical to effective healing. For the professional therapist focus is best established and maintained by making a *therapeutic contract*. This is also true for the nonprofessional healer, the reliable-friend.

What Is a Counseling Contract and How Do You Establish One?

When I left graduate school more than 30 years ago and began my professional career, I discovered I had learned a lot of useful counseling techniques and had a well-developed phil\sophy of treatment, but I found my counseling sessions were slow moving and filled with extraneous information I didn't know what to do with.

When asked, my supervisor suggested I needed to establish clear treatment contracts. This was, for me, a novel idea. It made sense, for as a counselor I was being benevolent, understanding and supportive, but I was not as effective as I would like. Even though the concept of a treatment contract was difficult for me to grasp at first, as I understood the process of making a treatment contract and its function, I found my counseling sessions became much more productive. Contracts provided me and my clients a clear way to keep focused on the problem at hand. With a treatment contract the seemingly irrelevant information became relevant.

Today I feel if there is only one thing a healer should know about providing useful counsel, it would be how to make a problem-solving contract. Yet for those who make such a contract, it becomes one of the most simple and logical techniques of counseling.

The functions of a problem-solving contract are:

- they keep both parties focused on the issue;
- they keep the responsibility for finding a solution on the person with the problem.

A problem-solving contract is established by having

the person presenting the problem answer three basic questions:

* How are you wanting to change (i.e. what problem do you want to solve)?
* How will you know when you have succeeded?
* How will I and others experience you as different because of the change you've made?

The answers to these three seemingly ordinary questions serve as a guide for both the persons providing and receiving counsel.

At first you may wonder what these three questions have to do with problem solving. It would seem someone turning to you with a problem does not want to change. However, they have a problem because they lack the skill and/or experience to solve it. Therefore, in order to solve the problem, they are needing to change their method of problem solving. Obviously the problem-solving method they have been using does not work or they would not be seeking help.

By having them focus on what they want to change, how they and I will recognize success and how others will know that they have succeeded in making the change, you are helping them focus on the skill and/or information they need. In the examples of contract making that follow, you will be able to see how this process works formally and informally. First, there are some general guidelines you will need to follow.

Each of the contract questions *must* be answered with *positive* statements. Often as you first address these questions, the person seeking counsel will offer *negative* answer like: I *won't* be unhappy, or I'll *stop* resenting my wife, or I *won't* be a doormat. Or they may give a *qualified* answer like: I'll be *less* frustrated, I won't be *as* lonely, I'll be *more* spontaneous.

Professional therapists find that negative and qualified statements do not provide workable contracts because they focus on *getting away from* something as opposed to *going on to* something. Contracts based on negative and qualified statements create internal paradoxes. For example: "Don't think about an elephant for the next 30 seconds." The paradox is, *the more you focus on what you want to get away from the more you reinforce it.*

Contracts stated positively, on the other hand, establish clear goals. To understand the difference between how negative and qualified statements affect you, say aloud: "When I have finished this book I'll be *less* confused about being a healer." Now, be aware of how you feel. Next say aloud: "When I have finished this book I'll know *what to do* as a healer." Pay attention to how you feel.

If you're like most people, making the first statement leaves you feeling vague and uncertain. The second statement, however, leaves you feeling clear, perhaps even hopeful. The first response is a qualified negative statement; whereas the second is a clear and positive statement that gives you a direction and a definite measurable goal. The former statement merely leaves you with a vague direction and an ambiguous goal.

To paraphrase Eric Berne, if the captain of an airplane comes on the P.A. system and says, "We're *going to try* to head this plane toward New York," you'll feel uncomfortable and you'd be well advised to get off the plane. While if the captain comes on the P.A. and says, "We're *going to* New York," you'll be likely to sit back and relax.

Qualified contracts are not clearly measurable. It is impossible to measure how much *less* and *more* are. I'll be *less* unhappy or I'll be *more* efficient does not provide either the person seeking counsel or the person offering counsel a clear route to success. Indeed, we can almost always be *less* or *more something*.

In order to negotiate an achievable contract, you'll first need to make the desires of the person seeking counsel *explicit, clear, direct* and *measurable*, such as, "I'll know what to do when I'm unhappy; I'll create experiences where I'm free to express myself spontaneously; I'll know what to do and how to get it done."

Positive statements like these provide achievable and measurable therapeutic goals which in turn allow both parties, the healer and the wounded, a way to assess how they are doing at any given point in the process of problem solving. They also give both the healer and the wounded a clear sense of victory when they succeed in problem-solving.

Clear positive answers to the three contract questions are invaluable aids in releasing your healing power. The following case presentation illustrates how to gain answers to these questions in a natural conversational manner.

Tom: "Well, I just needed to talk to someone about my situation with Sarah. I have tried to talk to her about it, but we can't seem to get anywhere. We just end up fighting."

Healer: "Let me get clear on what you want. How would you like things to be with Sarah?"

Tom: "Just normal, the way things should be."

Healer: "What's 'just normal'?"

Tom: "Well, *not* fighting, for one!"

Healer: "How would you state that in positive terms?"

Tom: "Being able to talk things over and seeing eye-to-eye."

Healer: "I see, so if you get what you want out of this conversation you will have a way to see eye-to-eye with Sarah and talk things over."

Tom: "If I could do that, it would be great."

Healer: "Well, if you did that how would your life be different?"

Tom: "I *wouldn't* be all torn up, calling you for help."

Healer: "How *would* you be and what *would* you be doing?"

Tom: "Well, I'd be happy, and spending my free time doing what I wanted to do and Sarah and I would be spending our time together enjoying each other rather than fighting."

Healer: "So, if you get what you want out of this conversation, you'll feel free to do what you want in your free time and you'll be spending time with Sarah appreciating and enjoying each other. Is that right?"

Tom: "Yeah, you've got it."

Healer: "Okay, let me review. The reason you want to talk to me is so you can find a way to see eye- to-eye with Sarah and be able to talk things over. If you accomplish that, you will be spending your free time doing what you want and you and Sarah will be enjoying each other. If you achieve these goals, how will I and others know that you've achieved your goals? How will you be different?"

Tom: "For one, I won"t be calling you for help."
Healer: "What will you be doing?"
Tom: "Well, I'll be calling you to talk about what is exciting and interesting to me, if I call at all."
Healer: "OK, I'm clear about what you want and how we both will know when you have achieved your wants. We have a contract. Now, tell me what's going on."

Some people who seek you out as a healer may resist the idea of making a formal problem-solving contract – whether their reasons vary from lack of trust to just plain ignorance. However, they have sought you out because they want help. They want a reliable-friend. When they resist making a clear statement, which occasionally happens, you'll need to establish a contract gradually and informally, letting the three basic questions at the beginning of the chapter guide your conversation.

Your contract doesn't have to be formal, but you do need explicit, positively stated goals. Professionals have been known to spend several months and have many conversations before getting a clear statement of what the client wants to accomplish. Clearly *it takes time to gain trust and it takes understanding to achieve clarity.* It's important to realize that just as the person presenting the problem wants to solve it, so you as a healer also want to be effective. Using the basic contract questions to guide you, no matter how long it takes, benefits both parties in the long run. Once while I was discussing this with a good friend named Liz, she raised hesitations about such a guideline of making a contract because it seemed too technical or jargony for her. She didn't think it would be something she could apply as she related to others as a reliable-friend.

Sometime later she called to say she wanted to discuss a serious problem about some disturbing concerns she had with her daughter. After briefly hearing what was going on with her daughter, I said I would be happy to talk with her further but felt it sounded as though we needed to schedule a time to talk rather than discuss her problem on the phone. She agreed so we set a time to talk. I then asked her what she wanted to get out of our conversation and she said she felt it would make her feel better to talk about this and sort through what she should do.

As you may recognize, we had already begun making a contract when I asked what she wanted to get out of our discussion. We found a time where we could stay focused and, according to our paradigm, my friend Liz was taking responsibility for finding her own solutions when she answered the question about what she wanted to get out of our talk.

Later she admitted that even before we had a chance to meet, she began to feel somewhat relieved because I, in acting as a reliable-friend, had calmly asked her to clarify what she was wanted to accomplish and then described what I thought was the best way we could deal with this problem. As soon as she was able to verbalize that what she needed most was to voice her concerns and come up with a plan, her anxiety level began to come down.

When we sat down to meet, we chatted briefly about other things and then she brought up her concern about her daughter Tanya. As we discussed Tanya, I asked her what her main worry was. She replied that she was apprehensive about some of her daughters recent choices and she wanted to make sure she and her daughter stayed in communication, and second, she wanted to feel good about the limits and discipline she was using.

That made sense to me so I shared my observations about how great I thought she was doing with Tanya and asked her how she would know if she had resolved her current issues. She said she hoped Tanya would still be able to confide in her when she needed to and that as a mother she would feel confident in her parenting choices.

When I queried about whether she thought there were going to be big changes for her and would she be different because of them, Liz said no, in fact she had good communication with Tanya up until now and usually she felt fairly confident as a parent. This assessment helped Liz to relax a little and remember that, in fact, she really did have the parenting skills to handle this well. Through talking, Liz came up with a plan for letting Tanya know she could come to her whenever she needed. She was also able to tell Tanya she still had limits and boundaries that she and Liz would negotiate as she matured.

Though the contract questions were answered in a very informal manner, I was still able to get answers to the three questions of: how are you wanting to change, how will you know when your successful and how will others experience you as different because of the change? This final question of how others would know that you had changed was not fully answered, but she and I both knew her confidence as a parent would be recognizable. In this normal contact, we were able to make a contract as two friends and it didn't become threatening or strained for Liz. When I pointed out to her how I had just used these questions to guide our conversation, she was able to see how we had in fact made a contract.

As healer, it is important to remember your need to be effective is as important as your friend's need is for help. Therefore, in getting a clear positive answer to the three contract questions, stick to your guns, but don't rigidly insist on your terms. For example, you may simply ask at an appropriate time: "What is your goal"? or "What is it you are wanting to get from talking to me?" The answers to these questions may give you *all* the information you need to feel satisfied you have a clear direct contract and you won't need to formalize it.

A counselee might respond, "I just want to know that someone understands." To which you can say, "How will that help?" As they answer your questions, you may want to restate their answers in positive terms like, "You want me to understand how you feel so that you will know that you have a friend with whom you can check things out." The important part of getting a problem-solving contract is for you as healer to have a clear, positive stated idea of what the person requesting your attention wants.

Sometimes you will want to establish a contract before you listen to their story. Or you might want to hear the story first and then establish a contract. Your intuition tells you the best order. However, *before* you begin searching for solutions, you're much better off if you have mutually agreed on, positively stated goals. As your work together and you begin to find solutions to the issues, you'll use your contract to keep on track.

You, the healer, will use the contract to direct your efforts by coming back to it periodically and asking questions like: "What does what you are talking about have to do with your contract?" and/or "How are you meeting the goals of your contract?" As counselors we find these are the questions we ask most frequently. As a general rule, whenever you are lost, confused, unclear or bewildered, it's fair to assume the person you are talking to is also lost, confused, unclear or bewildered. Returning to the contract will help you get back on track.

Technically, a contract is a mutual agreement to address a specific issue and these problem-solving contracts/agreements do three things: *First* they let the wounded define *the focus* of the work; *second,* they *establish agreements* to help the healer and the wounded stay on track; and *third*, they provide a clear way to *mark progress* and *recognize success.* A contract does for healing talk (therapy) the same thing a business agreement does for business dealings. It defines the terms people agree to follow.

Once you have a problem-solving contract, your work together becomes an mutually rewarding endeavor. Counseling is like a treasure hunt – each successful discovery gives clues to the next treasure until you finally discover the "pot of gold." On the other hand, without a clear agreement that defines focus and identifies success, the counseling process can be like wandering in a wilderness.

Things to Fix in Your Mind from this Chapter:

1. Freedom of focus is an important and little-recognized human power.

2. What you focus on and consort with, you become.

3. A contract answers three questions for both the healer and the wounded:

- ✷ What the wounded wants to accomplish,
- ✷ How they will know when they've got it,
- ✷ How you and others will recognize their success.

4. Contracts are invaluable in keeping focused on problem-solving.

5. The terms used to describe the process do not have to be formal, as long as they provide you clarity.

6. Go for the contract when it feels right, until then, listen and observe.

5

The Splinter in the Toe

Eric Berne, the father of Transactional Analysis, believed that therapy was too beneficial to humanity to be restricted to an elite wealthy clientele who could afford psychoanalysis. He developed a complete personality theory and treatment process based on simple, easily understood and applied concepts.

One of his objectives was to pass the treatment processes from the exclusive domain of the analyst's office to all helping professions. His theory and applications he called social psychiatry and his concepts of games, scripts and treatment contracts have influenced the whole field of psychotherapy. Berne's social psychiatry is based on the assumption that since psychic wounding occurs in a social setting, a social setting is the place psychic healing most effectively occurs.

Here we are taking his concept of passing the skills of therapy one step further because our aim is to put healing power in the hands of all who desire to release their healing power. It is important to note we are talking about healing, not analyzing – about using the natural healing power we all possess and use in normal caring conversations.

Eric Berne assumed that psychic cure was possible – a radical idea in his time. Cure was achieved by analyzing the transactions between people. By usual Transactional Analysis he demonstrated how people could break unhealthy transactional patterns and establish healthy behaviors through the process of therapy. His form of therapy is based on two basic assumptions:

1. Human beings are OK, and
2. You can understand and change behaviors that are self-limiting.

His motto was, "get well first and find out why you were ill later."

Best known for concepts like I'm OK you're OK, contracts, strokes, games and scripts, Dr. Berne also emphasized the lesser-known, but pivotal, concept – "The Splinter In the Toe." Basically this says: A guy accidentally gets a splinter in his toe. The splinter causes an infection and the infection causes swelling and soreness. He begins to limp – which causes his muscles to tighten, giving him muscle spasms. The infection, caused by the splinter, spreads through the system and he develops a fever.

Stumbling into a doctor's office, he has an infection, aching muscles and a fever. The doctor looks him over and says, "Wow, this is serious. Your whole system is involved. I can do treatment. It may take a long time and there's is no guarantee it will work." So, the guy goes for a second opinion. The next doctor says, "Well, you have an infection from a splinter in the toe. I'll remove the splinter, give you a shot of penicillin and you'll be back to normal in 48 hours."

The way the first doctor practiced medicine Berne stated was the standard psychiatric approach at that time. The way the second doctor practiced medicine was the way that Berne taught Transactional Analysts to practice therapy. Like the second doctor, we as healers are looking for the splinter in the toe. Once we find it we can assist the person in removing it and help them find the proper prescription to alleviate the suffering and restore natural health.

Finding the Splinter in the Toe

You will not be functioning as a healer long before you discover recurring themes come up as you talk with most people about problems. Even though the situations someone presents may at first appear to be unique, as time goes on you'll soon recognize that you keep coming back to familiar themes.

Hearing this repetition, you'll have that, here-we- go-again feeling. Don't be discouraged. Each retelling of someone's story provides more information. In fact, Gestalt therapists compare therapy to peeling an onion – layer by layer. Many times, you'll have had to hear several different versions of the *same* story before you begin to see the pattern or locate the splinter in the toe. You'll come to recognize that each telling is an attempt to discover the source of the wound.

Returning again and again to the same scenario was called a "repetition compulsion" by Sigmund Freud and "advancing a script, or playing a game" by Eric Berne. Whatever you call it, this is a means of pointing to the splinter in the toe. Simply to label it in some diagnostic or judgmental way is a mistake. The task of a healer is to assist someone in seeing the pattern and finding the cause – the splinter in the toe.

Walter, a highly skilled engineer, called for help three times in six months. The first time he was depressed. His company was restructuring. Since he knew he had not been as productive as he could have been, he was sure he would be laid off. The second call was about his son who had gotten in trouble at school. Again he reported he was depressed because, "If I'd just been a better father he wouldn't have these problems." The third time he called, he just didn't seem to be getting anywhere in life and was wondering what he had done wrong to be at this stage of life and not have gotten any farther.

On the surface Walter's problems seemed ordinary enough. Each time we talked them through he felt a little better and was able to take some steps to solve his immediate problem. However, as I thought about the common thread in Walter's calls, I realized that he had a pattern of making bad situations worse by blaming himself – and blaming himself for every adversity he encountered in life exacerbated his pain and fed his depression.

For an analyst, identifying self-blaming as the splinter in the toe (i.e. the way he made bad situations worse) is cause for depth investigation. However, with all due apologies to the analytic tradition, once the analysis is done and the individual fully understands the "pathological roots" of his dilemma, the cure is found in changing behavior: abandoning the old behavior and taking up a new behavior.

For the reliable-friend who identifies the splinter in the toe, analysis is not a good option nor is it an option they are trained to pursue. The friend, however, analyzes situations and patterns. As healers we simply make observations and suggest more productive behaviors. This is the most natural and common form of healing. In Walter's case my conclusion was: "It seems to me that blaming yourself is a pattern. In the situations we've talked about, this is not only counter-productive, but it exacerbates the pain."

I suggested to Walter, "For the next few weeks, stop yourself any time you are aware of self-blaming. Change your focus to something to help yourself. Find something more productive, rewarding or more enjoyable and let me know how things go." This type of intervention fulfills Eric Berne's admonition, "Get well first, find out why later – if you have the time and interest."

Options for Intervening

Therapists have at their disposal three major ways to intervene: *counsel, analysis* and *confrontation*. Counseling interventions are the easiest for people to understand and profit from because they provide behavioral options. Analysis is more difficult because it is designed to connect past experiences with present dilemmas and in the process goes back into the whys and wherefores from the past – conscious and unconscious. Confrontation is difficult for clients to understand and assimilate because it is one person's judging another to be doing wrong. Consequently confrontation is often mistaken for attack.

When attacked, we naturally defend ourselves. "Why are you doing ... (something that hasn't or won't work)?" is frequently our first question when we are confronting. Seldom are the *why* questions helpful. As children we all learned to give *because* answers to *why* questions. Indeed, confronting first and analyzing second is exactly the wrong order in which to proceed if we want to be effective healers. It is one reason why many of our best efforts to help fall flat. The way I explain it in workshops is, "if confrontation were healing, the whole world would be well." This is usually met with amused nods of recognition.

Likewise, to be an effective healer in most normal interpersonal exchanges, it is a good idea to give up analyzing behavioral patterns and simply observe what is going on between you and the person seeking your counsel. Just as seldom does it do much good to tell others how they are messing up, so pointing out parallels from the past doesn't offer much help. Such activities are better left to the professional.

What is beneficial in normal human relations is helping people focus on productive behaviors and possible solutions. This requires you to be objective rather than judgmental or analytical. When you are objective about what you are hearing, you help people discover dysfunctional patterns and assist them in developing a plan for new and more productive action.

Therefore, when you think you have identified the *splinter in the toe*, confrontation and analysis may not be your most productive interventions. Offering thoughtful and caring counsel and mutually searching out promising options and possible new behaviors is truly helpful. This is what good friends consistently do for each. Both analysis and confrontation are normal in the ongoing give-and-take of conversation. When we are in a healer/wounded mode these two interventions are not very productive tools. Analysis can lead to paralysis and confrontation may lead to a rift in the friendship.

Looking back at Walter's situation, when the going got tough, *his* self-defeating behavior was blaming himself and putting himself down. As we consulted, neither of us were sure how this pattern had developed. However following the splinter in the toe theory, it was not important to know where the pattern began. What Walter needed to do was to was give himself support when the difficulties arose. Instead he was giving himself a *bad time*. No wonder he was depressed. As he changed his behavior, he removed the splinter from his toe – the habit of self blaming.

In another incident at a senior citizen's community meeting Helen, 68 and retired, asked her friend Joani to go for coffee. At the coffee shop Helen confided in her that she was worried and depressed because she and her husband had invested most of their savings in their daughter and son-in-law's business venture. Not only had the business gone belly-up, but the daughter and son-in-law were getting a divorce. Helen was frightened, angry and worried.

Joani, listening to the story and feeling Helen's pain and anxiety, realized she could offer sympathy, reassurance, be outraged at the children's thoughtlessness – or she could offer counsel. Counsel would be something that would help Helen through this troubled time. Feeling sorry for her or being indignant wouldn't provide much more help than is held in the old aphorism, "misery loves company." So recognizing she was being called on to be a healer, Joani listened closely and crafted a response she thought would help Helen, for in telling the story Helen made it clear their dilemma was a result of real caring about her daughter's well-being.

After absorbing the details of Helen's story, Joani asked her if the reason for lending her daughter the money in the first place had been based on love and caring. Helen agreed that was her motivation. Joani then inquired if she would do the same thing again if she thought it would help them. Helen said yes.

By probing with these questions Joani helped Helen see herself as a caring mother. As a result of her answers, Helen's perspective shifted. Instead of chiding herself as someone who had done something foolish, she began to perceive herself as a caring, loving mother. With this shift in focus, Helen also began to recall how she had overcome other bad situations in her life. Helen thanked Joani for helping regain her perspective and they both ended up feeling better about themselves as a result of this encounter. Had Joani merely commiserated with Helen, they may have both left feeling depressed and no healing would have transpired.

It's important to realize that Joani's interventions were based upon hearing Helen's request as a need for healing. Joani had intuitively gone for the splinter in the toe–the loss of self-esteem the situation induced. As a result of using the processes outlined in this book–thinking of herself as a healer and listening to Helen's story–Joani was able to find the real wound and be a reliable-friend.

To review what Joani did:

- She thought of herself as a healer.
- She owned the healing power of healthy inter-dependent relationships.
- She listened to the story.
- She kept her focus on what needed healing.
- She discovered and removed the *splinter in the toe.*

Ideas from this Chapter to Fix in Your Mind:

1. Your intuition is one of your most powerful tools.

2. You are always looking for the splinter in the toe, no matter what else is going on.

6

Doing the Right Thing

Since our lives are lived in a wounding/healing context, even the most withdrawn and reclusive person in the world can hardly avoid attachments and implicit, unsolicited requests for healing. We have interdependent relationships and we use them consciously and unconsciously as sources of healing hurts and celebrating the victories in our lives. Therefore, we are well advised to have some clear ideas of what to do when our healing power is sought.

What Is a Healthy Healer?

Simply stated, a healthy healer is someone who is *tough* and *kind* and who knows how to say *yes* and *no*. *Tough* means that they *hang in there* using their best judgment and stick with friends when they are troubled. *Kind* means that they *operate out of genuine caring*. Reliable-friends are also people who say *yes* and *no* to themselves and others as they realistically assess their abilities and limitations. All of us know and admire people who are tough and kind. These are those whom we know we can rely on to "speak the truth in love." Holding ourselves to these standards helps us become resources for healing.

Being tough and kind and learning to say yes and no to ourselves and others does not mean that we will do it right all the time. Indeed, we will become over-extended – have times when we say *no* and wish we had said *yes*, or vice versa. However, as we learn to say yes and no to ourselves and each other, the times when we err become less frequent.

It is also important to recognize and acknowledge that we always strive to do our best. We have tried to do our best, even in those times when we discover we have erred, have made poor judgments or our best has proven inadequate. Since we never set out to mess things up, make a poor judgement or to let someone down, even though there are times when we do, it does not logically follow that we haven't done our best. We have. We have just failed to assess our capability, resources or energy – proving again the bon mot that: Good judgment comes from experience, and experience comes from bad judgment.

Therefore, a healthy healer is someone who is *tough* and *kind* and who has learned or is learning to say *yes* and *no* to ourselves and others.

Right Things to Do When Functioning as a Healer

It's impossible to list *all* the specific appropriate things we can do as healers. Each time you can help someone heal the wounds of life, you are in a unique situation. Even if you have been through similar incidents many times before, you have never been through it with *this person* in *this time* and *this place*. Therefore, the best we can do is to give general directions that we have discovered or guidelines we can follow:

- ✳ Think of yourself as a healer.
- ✳ Recognize coos and cries when you hear them.
- ✳ Listen to others stories until you understand their situation and feel their experience.
- ✳ Establish clear positive and measurable agreed upon goals develop an eye for "the splinter in the toe."
- ✳ Set realistic expectations for yourself.

Steps to Take as a Healer

(Handy, Helpful, Household Hints)

Follow Process:

When functioning as a healer you can either lead or follow the process. It is most effective to let the *person seeking help lead*. Whenever the wounded invite you into their world, they are the experts, *albeit,* often confused expert. If you follow their story and ask for points of clarification, when things are unclear, you are following the process.

Understanding what it means to *lead* the process

makes it easier to understand what we mean to *follow* process. For the healer, leading is having in mind some forgone conclusion you would like the person you are counseling to come to. When this is the case, even when you may be absolutely accurate in your assessment and the person seeking your counsel agrees with your conclusions, it's usually not a useful way to proceed because you are thinking *for* the person rather than *with* them.

Thinking *with* the person you counsel is most effective in the long run. While it may seem expeditious to think *for* someone and give them or lead them to an answer, you will have failed to help them develop their skills at problem solving. Further, when you think *for* someone rather than *with* them, you may unconsciously create a dependency. Generally, when this happens, eventually the day comes when either you or they resent the dependence.

Following the process does not mean you shouldn't share your insight, only that you need to *own* (take full responsibility) for your insights. A statement like: "What I think is going on here is ...," is frequently useful. Certainly it is more useful than if you hold back your idea or insight and play some cat-and-mouse game to get the person to come to a conclusion you have in mind. It is also more effective than saying: "What you're doing is ...." By being forthright about what you are hearing and owning your perceptions, you are opening dialogue in a status equal fashion. It is a truism that: "The quality of the dialogue determines the quality of the relationship."

Following process does not mean that you can't be

directive. When you experience things getting scattered it is often good to be directive. You can say: "I'd like to stay with that for a moment, to hear a little more detail about this, to explore what that is about, to know how you think this situation will resolve, etc." With statements like this, you are being directive but you are *not* leading. You are simply being up-front about what you think *you* need to be useful. This is a fine distinction, but an important one.

One final warning about the advantages of following rather than leading: When you lead, even if you are dead right, the person you are helping may have some sense of being one-upped. If this happens, you ever so slightly change the enterprise from one of mutual problem-solving (working together) to competitive problem solving (mine is better than yours). In competitions there can be only one winner. With mutual problem-solving everyone can be a winner.

Successful healing ultimately ends with both parties having a sense of winning–recall how Joani and Helen ended. Both walked away feeling good about themselves. Had Joani one-upped Helen, she would likely have been left feeling one-down.

Don't Tolerate Abuse:

Abuse can be generalized to making someone not OK. People in pain frequently abuse themselves, as was illustrated in Walter's situation of self-blaming. People most commonly abuse themselves by labeling past behaviors as stupid, dumb, foolish, etc. Abusive statements made by yourself or others hurt. It is natural to protect ourselves when we encounter an abuse/hurt. This protecting of self is being defensive. Feeling we have to defend ourselves covers a hurt and makes us less accessible for healing interventions.

As a healer, it is important to confront someone gently each time you hear a potentially abusive self-assessment. A straightforward, "I'll go along with the idea that what you did worked out poorly, but I won't go along with the idea that you're stupid, dumb or foolish." Such statements made by a counselor lets the person know you will not collude with their self-abuse. Further, it helps them to realize you are on their side and are interested in their health and well-being.

Occasionally, you'll find you are spending a great deal of time confronting self-abusing statements. When this happens, it is good to make an agreement with the person *not* to use such statements during the times you are together or during the time that they are focusing on problem-solving. Statements like, "Will you agree not to call yourself names in my presence?" "Would you be willing to think of a non-abusive way to describe yourself or others during the time we are working to solve this problem?" establishes that you, as a healer, will not tolerate abuse.

Confronting self-abuse is a delicate and complex issue because your action may be misinterpreted as a judgment. To make sure you are understood and that you do not threaten your alliance with your counselee, it is a good idea to make an explicit agreement about confronting abuse. Early on in the relationship you may need to state you would like to make an agreement that if and when you hear or suspect self-abuse, you will bring it up. Say something like:

1. "My experience has taught me that abuse of yourself is not helpful in finding a solution to problems. Therefore, I would like to make an agreement with you that I will confront anything I think might be self-abusive and trust you will make every effort to describe yourself and your behaviors in non-judgmental terms."

2. "Self-abuse is something we do unconsciously. I would like for us to agree that I should point it out when I hear something I think smacks of self-abuse. Is that OK with you?"

Coincidentally, by making such an agreement, you have created a paradoxical situation (technically called paradoxical intention) for even if the people you work with refuse to make such an agreement, you have sensitized them to the counter-productive quality of self-abuse. Once sensitized, they begin to hear their own self-abuse whenever they do it. Therefore, they begin to hear it for what it is – a self-defeating process.

Those who put themselves down or select harsh, negative, judgmental words to describe themselves and their actions are subtly reinforcing their own wounding (incapacitation). Breaking this habit in and of itself is healing.

Abuse hurts, no matter whom it comes from or no

matter or whom it is directed toward. People who abuse themselves, their mates, parents, bosses, etc. verbally or physically, are using potentially damaging ways to express concern, frustration, anger, hurt, etc. By refusing to let abusive statements go without confronting them, you are helping them stay focused and be solution-oriented.

No Blaming:

Blaming is like swearing: *It sounds like hell and doesn't do a damn bit of good.* Finding a guilty party or unfortunate situation/circumstance to blame may lead to righteous indignation, but it does not necessarily lead to healing.

Instead of ascribing blame, you need to keep yourself and the person you counsel focused on *why* and *how* things went wrong and *what* to do about it. For example, perhaps the person you are helping trusted the wrong person. It is helpful to discover what led a person to trust someone who violated their trust, but it is not helpful to launch a tirade about that person.

Once you both have concluded why they've trusted the wrong person, they are likely to be more judicious, cautious and perceptive about whom they trust in future situations. Such information allows them to gain from the experience. However, if you only establish that a hurt was someone's fault, the wounded person may feel righteous and indignant, but they have not developed their ability to avoid such mistakes in the future.

Some years ago Marla, a very able administrator who holds a responsible job in government but has terrible relationships with men, stopped to visit. She was wearing a T-shirt emblazoned with the slogan: "*Why Do I Always Fall for Chicken-Shits on Ego Trips?*" I asked her about it. She said she had ordered it out of a book by the same title. "This is what I always do, so I thought I might as well advertise."

To the best of my knowledge, she is still following the same pattern. Blaming herself for poor selection and even advertising it has not led to healing. If I were to be a reliable-friend and she were to request my help, I would need to help her reverse her pattern of blaming and begin to use her considerable skill to discover *why* she does what she does in the selection of men.

When in Doubt, Punt:

The strategy of the punt is to keep the responsibility for finding the solution in the hands of the person with the problem. A punt is a strategic move in football used when a football team cannot make adequate yardage to advance toward the goal. The strategy is to kick the ball deep into the other team's territory, switching from offense to defense and hoping to gain possession of the ball in a more advantageous position.

In helping others, the strategy of the punt is the same as in football. When you aren't getting anywhere in a counseling situation or you become confused, lost or frustrated it always a good idea to punt–to ask the person you are working with what to do. You can say, "I'm stuck, what do you think is going on here? What do you make of that? or Where do we go from here?" These questions are almost always productive when you don't have any idea what to do next.

Just as a football team will attempt to place the ball deep in the other team's territory whenever they calculate that they can't make any gains, so the healer needs to know that he can place the responsibility for direction on the person seeking counsel. Not surprisingly, when you use the strategy of the punt in counseling, the person presenting the problem will frequently come up with a productive idea of what to do and where to head.

Recently I was discussing with a friend his dilemma about taking an anti-anxiety medication. His situation was complex and I was not his therapist, yet he wanted to talk to me. Since I have known him for a long time and felt that he needed a reliable-friend as well as a therapist, I agreed to discuss his medication dilemma with him – even though usually I wouldn't have done this. In our conversation, it wasn't long until I was overwhelmed with the details of the conflict between the medical advice provided by his MD and the clinical advice provided by his therapist. He just didn't know whose advice to follow.

Since I realized that offering additional advice would add to his confusion, I asked, "What do *you* want to do?" He said he didn't know what was the right thing to do. "No," I said. "What do *you* want to do?"

"Well," he answered, "What I *want* to do is call the doctor and tell him that I want him and my therapist to confer."

I responded, "That sounds like a good idea to me."

He did and called back and thanked me for helping

him out of his dilemma. In truth he helped himself – I had merely punted!

Use Humor:

Problem-solving is serious business, but not so serious that you need lose your sense of humor – albeit that this is easy to lose when you are in the middle of a predicament. Frequently I comment, "When we have a problem we talk more and more about less and less." Humor helps restore perspective. It lightens us up and reminds us there is more in life than just difficulties. As a healer, never be afraid to inject some humor into the situation. You'll find that it can be healing.

The only caution I would offer about the use of humor is to make sure your humorous statements are not at someone's expense – and never tolerate *gallows humor* which means laughing at something that is self- destructive or self-abusive. The idea of gallows humor comes from the man about to be hanged who says, "I've never had a necktie like this one."

Don't Pathologize:

Our age is an age of psychological analysis. Most people have an informal vocabulary of pathological terms they use to label behaviors they find troubling or do not understand. Labeling is seldom helpful. Professionally, diagnostic labels are used to prescribe treatments that have proven to be effective with various psychological disorders. However, the general public has picked up on such labels and uses them in a judgmental way rather than a prescriptive way.

To be a reliable-friend, it is not helpful to use labels, no matter how well-intended. Recently, I was talking with a friend and said casually that he was a "good paranoid." What I meant to communicate was that he examined things thoroughly before he made a decision. What happened was that he took what I said as a negative statement about him and later became troubled by my statement. What was meant as a compliment caused him stress because I chose to use a technical term indiscriminately to describe a behavior.

Using diagnostic terms when you are counseling is dangerous at best and disastrous at worst. Using such terms is likely to cause the person seeking counsel to feel one-down. Most people don't realize that diagnostic labels were developed to prescribe treatments that were effective when certain symptoms were present. Diagnostic labels are based on statistical analysis and are designed to be prescriptive. Using them to simply label behaviors impedes the counseling process.

Build on Health:

A sage has said, "It is easier to take up new behavior than to give up old behavior." When we are offering counsel it is most helpful to build on health, instead of giving in to our tendency "to think more and more about less and less." Problems have a tendency to dominate our attention. A reliable-friend is someone who sees much more than the problem. Therefore, it is important to keep pointing out to the counselee the areas where they are functioning well. This helps them to maintain their psychological balance and bring their full resources to the problem-solving process.

While it is not a good idea to minimize or discount the significance of the problem, it is equally inappropriate to see only the problem. A reliable-friend is someone who helps you stay in touch with all your capacities and abilities. While you are focusing on problem-solving, it is always a good idea to recognize and identify (stroke) healthy behaviors as they come up. Positive statements in the counseling session are always in order.

The Curse of Grandiosity

To be an effective healer and remain healthy it is important to be aware of the danger of grandiosity – which arises from the assumption that we have no limits and/or possess superhuman powers. Grandiose ideas are like:

- We should have a solution for all the dilemmas that come to us.
- When we hear about trouble and tribulation we must do something about it.
- Whether someone likes us or not is of our doing rather than their choosing. And,
- Since we can see what is happening, we must fix it.

The saying, "My swimming pool is filled with piranhas – I guess I should go swimming because someone has to feed the piranhas," exemplifies the danger of grandiosity.

Operating under the curse of grandiosity inevitably

ends in incapacitation. When we hold unrealistic expectations for ourselves we will eventually crash. When Bill thinks he can or has to solve Ted's problems, he is making Ted's needs more important than his own. Whenever people make other's issues more important than their own, it isn't long until they become overloaded and implode. In Bill's case, he will either become exhausted, resent Ted, feel worthless or experience some equally debilitating outcome.

The alternative to operating with unrealistic expectations, of course, is operating with realistic ones. As a healer, the only authentic expectation you can hold for yourself is to be a reliable-friend. Just as it is reasonable to be a "good-enough" parent and impossible to be a "perfect" parent, so it is irrational to be a savior and realistic to be a reliable-friend–the kind that strive to assess both their skills and resources accurately. Reliable- friends unapologetically acknowledge their personal limits. Realistically, you may have neither the time, inclination or ability acquiesce to some requests.

At the times when you do feel you have the resources and time to function as a healer, your expectation of yourself should be no grander than to be a reliable-friend–someone who knows and clearly states their limits. Of course this also means sticking with the other until they find an adequate resource or solution that heals their hurt whenever they can. Also a reliable-friend is someone who is available to celebrate with them when they have achieved a victory.

When we accept the invitation to function as a healer

it is important to assess ourselves accurately. One way you can accomplish this assessment is by asking yourself questions such as:

1. Am I up to meeting this request?
2. Do I have the skill and talent to be helpful?
3. Am I willing to say when I feel I'm in over my head?
4. Do I have enough connection with this person to bear the pain and struggle of problem solving?

These questions always need to be in the forefront of our minds if we are to remain healthy healers.

7

Ending and Checking Up

Ending

How you end sessions is critically important to the process of healing and to the well-being of the healer. A healer who does not end sessions well will eventually become cynical and/or burned out. A sure sign you are not ending well is when you find you are thinking about the person's problems after sessions. This is called after-burn. After-burn almost always leads to cynicism and/or resentment – which in turn means you're likely to abandon the person and feel like a failure as a healer. Knowing how to end so that you don't burn out is *your* responsibility.

The cardinal rule for ending is to always conclude by placing the responsibility for the problem back on the person with the problem. You can close a discussion by saying something like: "Let me know how you handle that;" or "Let me know what you decide to do about that." As you become proficient at this, you'll find most of the time you'll walk away from a consultation feeling you've been helpful. Ending by placing the *full* responsibility squarely where it belongs closes the session.

When you end a session well it does not linger in your mind–not that you won't have some insights between your talks. You will. But you won't be pondering, worrying or obsessing about problems brought up in the session.

Concluding with a transaction that clearly fixes the responsibility for problem solving on the person presenting the problem does two things:

- By implication, it confronts the counselee with the fact they have the ability to solve the problem.
- It acknowledges the limits of reliable friendship.

It is important that the person seeking counsel know both of these facts, for they must be convinced you believe in their ability to solve the problem, and they need to understand there are clear limits to what you as healer can and will do.

By developing your skills at ending sessions effectively, you are also teaching good life-management skills through your example. Eric Berne says therapy is over when a client says, "Is that all?" and the therapist can honestly say, "Yes, that's all, and you can handle it." In counseling you will need to be point out that they have the ability to solve their problems in each session.

You'll find that in informal counseling situations it is easy to run on and on. This makes knowing when and how to end all the more important. Therefore, you need to set your own rules for ending and keep them clearly in mind. A colleague of mine ends sessions whenever the client has a clear victory, he is hungry, tired or he has spent 20 minutes and not gotten anywhere. You will need to establish *your* personal rules for ending. Remember, it is the healer's responsibility to set limits and establish clear boundaries.

A Word of Warning

Effective counseling is "heady"–it feels good, is rewarding and is ego inflating. For these reasons it is easy to lose sight of why you are doing it in the first place. You are not doing it to feel better about yourself nor do you want to create dependency. Therefore, ending when the counselee has made a clear victory is a primary goal. Such endings help to keep your energy serving the person you are consulting and not your vanity.

Your rules about ending need to be clear and explicit. Two simple, but sometimes hard-to-follow, rules are:

- Conclude by placing the responsibility for the problem on the counselee.
- If possible, stop when the counselee has a clear victory.

The first rule is easy to be hard-and-fast about–but not so the second. In times when you do not have a clear victory, a good policy is to have the person you are working with review what has happened and ask what they have gained and what they think the next step should be. "What have we accomplished today, and what do you want to do next?" is a good question to ask when you are ready to end and/or when you don't have a clear victory. Even when you have a clear recognition of an achievement, it is a good idea to have the person presenting the problem state the success as you conclude your talk.

Healers Need Healers

The more you recognize yourself as a healer and respond positively to requests for healing, the more you'll need to have your own healers to confer with – and this needs to be in the plural because it is important to have several people available to you. First, because one person is not always readily accessible; and second, because different people bring varied areas of expertise.

No psychotherapist worthy of the name would do therapy without competent supervisors and/or peers with whom they can discuss personal and professional issues. Thus whenever you assume the role of a healer, you will need your own personal consultants to turn to for guidance and advise. Ideally these will be persons with whom you can comfortably discuss both your personal and professional issues.

This book originated from our ongoing consultations with each other about our issues – personal and professional. Since we each have chosen to be healers in our own realms, we realized that what we do for each other as we discuss personal and professional issues is more than just discussing techniques and skills. We are helping each other keep balance in our lives amidst our busy schedules and perplexing problems. Working together writing these chapters not only enriches our lives, it also provides us better access to one another's skills.

Why We Need Our Own Healers

Robert Phillips, MD, succinctly points out that as human beings we have two primary systems: a *providing* system and a *receiving* system. When we are working with and for others – giving our full attention to their issues – we are in a providing system. When we are consulting with our healers we are in our receiving system.

In order to have optimum psychological health, we need to spend approximately equal amounts of time in each system. Too much time in our providing system shows up in both our dispositions and our bodies – we become grouchy and achy. Too much time in our receiving system causes us to become discontented, dull and lethargic.

Persons who see themselves as healers are commonly those who are prone to spend more time in their providing systems than in their receiving systems. Having personal healers helps us to balance out our providing and receiving needs.

As we deliberately call on others to be healers, we shift into a receiving posture. Even though we might be talking a-mile-a-minute and be having all kinds of insights, still we are in our receiving posture. At the end of a productive consultation with *our* healer, we should feel in better balance than when we began, even though we may have been reviewing a knotty issue.

Additionally, our healers need to be people that will be tough and kind – someone with whom we would feel free to ask questions like, "What do you see *me* doing that contributes to my problem, ineffectiveness or the issue I am presenting?" The healers we choose should be those who know us well enough to chasten us if they observe us doing something that is sabotaging our effectiveness or well-being.

Selecting your personal healers carefully is essential to being a healthy healer. Most frequently they will be colleagues – people we invite into our lives just like any other special friend. Sometimes we will make formal and contractual invitations – explicit agreements with persons to be our consultant. Sometimes our healers just naturally evolve. Whichever the case, it is a good idea to make a formal agreement with them to function as our healer.

One of the primary healers in my life and I made a mutual agreement 30 years ago as we were on a plane flying to a convention. We had been in training together and were en route to our first international convention as fully certified therapists, when he turned to me and said, "I would like to make an agreement for us to be resources to each other. I will give you an hour anytime you need it and you'll give me an hour anytime I need it."

Through the years we have used this agreement about equally. A surprise benefit, as a result of our agreement, has been that just knowing we could always call the other and arrange a meeting at any time has given us an added sense of security as we practiced our profession.

Right now, make a promise to yourself to select three to five personal healers. Arrange a time to meet with each of them and discuss how you can use each other to keep in balance and make an explicit formal agreement.

Confidentiality

Confidentiality is critical to being an effective counselor. This is usually assumed when you enter the domain of intentional talking; however, it is important to state explicitly, "This conversation is confidential." If it is left unstated, you may have differing assumptions. When this happens an unintentional violation of confidentiality may occur – and when you do this you damage the friendship.

Some things you will want to refuse to keep confidential – such items as fall into the broad category of hurting self or other. Here again you will need to state explicitly you will help the person as a reliable-friend, but you will not collude with anything that is potentially *self-* or *other-*destructive. On those rare times when something injurious is disclosed in your intentional talking, you will need to address it directly.

If it involves either self-inflicting or other-inflicting ideas or plans, you will need to stay with the your counselee until you get them into the hands of a competent professional – taking them to a therapist, physician, clergyperson or the like. While this is an awesome responsibility and such situations are always stressful, it is important to remember they turned to you for healing – so on the deepest level they do not want to hurt themselves or others and that is why they have reached out for help.

Lethal Issues

If the person you are counseling has suicidal thoughts, you will need to say to them calmly and directly, "Don't kill yourself." If the thoughts expressed are homicidal you will need to say to them calmly and directly, "Don't kill ... (the person they are having homicidal thoughts toward)." Again, you then have the responsibility to stay with them until you can get competent, professional help.

By giving them this specific order in a calm and direct manner, you help them connect with the healthy part of them–the part that wants to be whole and healthy. By being unruffled, you directly neutralize their "crazy" thinking. Because you are a reliable-friend who cares, your words will stay with them as they get the necessary help to get beyond their desperation.

Sometimes the person will not bring their destructive thoughts up, but you will have an intuitive feeling that they are having suicidal or homicidal fantasies. When you have these intuitive flashes, it is important to bring them up and ask directly: "Are you having suicidal or homicidal thoughts?" If they answer yes, give them a quiet directive, "Don't kill yourself," or "Don't kill ...." Such statements will offer both of you protection.

Again, once you have made such a statement, you will want to stay with them until you get them connected with a competent professional. If, when asked about suicidal or homicidal thoughts, they answer "no" and you still feel concern, just to be on the safe side, make these gentle injunctions: Don't kill yourself. Don't kill anyone. As they say in suicide prevention circles, "Suicide, [homicide also applies here] is a permanent solution to a temporary problem."

To reiterate: When self- or other-destructive thoughts are brought up it can be extremely stressful to you as a healer. Therefore, it is important that you have your own healers to reach out to on a moment's notice.

Be Realistic

Establishing and maintaining healthy interdependent relationships improves life and makes it more meaningful. This is not to imply that you will achieve a life filled only with ease and joy. Awareness of the reality that wounding and healing are parts of our pilgrimage makes us sensitive to the pain and struggle we all share.

The Creator, in ultimate wisdom, made us with the ability to heal the psychic wounds that result from our free will and from living in a less than optimal (toxic) environments. Just as physical wound healing and immune responses occur naturally and can only be enhanced with the use of such things as nutrition, rest, antiseptics and antibiotics, so the healing provided through intentional talking in interdependent relationships occurs naturally and spontaneously and can be enhanced with skilled caring.

The question of whether or not you will assume the role of healer as a conscious choice is an important one. As you recognize that you will be called on to be a healer whether you want to or not, you become increasingly aware that you must make deliberate decisions to develop and use your skill.

By Way of Review

A contract for treatment creates a temporary inequality so that a greater equality is ultimately possible. To understand this, it is important to see the whole process of healing in an idealized form—because no situation works out exactly according to the blueprint. However, let's paint an idealized scenario.

Two persons, one hurting and one a healer, originally come together as equals, albeit from varied life conditions. They make a contract for problem-solving. One expresses the issue, the other agrees to guide in the exploration for solutions. Ideally, they'll conclude each session with the wounded taking more and more responsibility for solving their problem. When this is ultimately resolved, the contract is fulfilled–and then the same two meet as equals with greater possibilities for intimacy, usefulness and healthy interdependence.

For the times you say yes to requests for counsel, the following pages contain a checklist you can use to help yourself stay focused and hone your skills.

Checklist Instructions:

Once a week set aside 30 minutes to review your recent healing actions. Recall a time during the past week when your counsel was requested.

Ask yourself these questions:

1. Was I thinking of myself as a healer when I was approached?

2. Was I thinking of myself as a healer as our conversation began?

3. Did I clearly state my energy, time and skill availability as we began?

4. Did I get a clear positively-stated contract?

   - How was the person wanting to grow and develop?
   - How did they say they would recognize their success?
   - What would be different about their behavior?
   - What would be different about their disposition?
   - How would I and others know they had changed?
   - Did I make the terms of the contract clear to my counselee?

5. What were the major feelings expressed and did I bear in mind what was the natural healthy resolving action for that feeling?

anger – redress   fear – protection
grief – comfort   joy – companionate-celebration

6. As I listened was I:

bored – intrigued – lost – insightful – in parallel-process?

7. How did I use my listening skills to help them?

8. Did I detect the splinter in the toe? ___yes ___no

9. Did the person I was working with detect the splinter in the toe? ___yes ___no

10. If you answered yes to either of the previous questions:

* What was the splinter?
* What did I do about it?

11. If you answered no to the splinter questions, do you now have a hunch as what it might be? ___yes ___no

* What's your hunch and what do you plan to do with it?
* What is your intuition telling you?

12. What interventions did I use?

Confrontation ___% Analysis ___% Counsel ___%

13. Did I avoid grandiosity?

14. Did I follow process? ___ yes ___% ___ no ___%

15. Did I confront abuse? ___ yes ___% ___ no ___%

16. Did I avoid getting drawn into blaming?

17. Did I use the strategy of the punt when we were stuck?

18. Did I use non-harmful humor?

19. Did I end by placing the responsibility upon the person I was counseling?

20. What are the issues I plan to talk over with my healer?

21. As you review this checklist, are there areas you need to reread in the book? If so, list them or mark them in the book.

8

What to Do If?

While it is impossible to give a detailed description of how to apply the healing processes we have presented to all the situations you will face, in this section we address some of the basic situations that come up as you exercise your healing power. This section is a reference guide to use when you are actually in the middle of giving counsel to someone.

What to Do If:

Someone Develops an Over-Attachment

Occasionally the person you are working with will become overly-attached to you. This happens for a variety of reasons. It may stem from their unmet needs or they may not have an adequate support system in their life so begin to cling to you emotionally because you are available. This may also be a life pattern for them. When overattachment happens, it's best to first ask yourself if you have inadvertently contributed to it. Occasionally, we unconsciously become "the answer person" for someone.

If, after reflecting on the exchanges you've had, you sense this pattern developing, you can begin by going over the checklist we have provided. It may be that you need to rework your contract and say something as simple as "What are *your* goals and how do *you* plan to achieve them?" This type of transaction gently shifts your counselee back into taking responsibility for solving their own problems. As you begin to correct a developing dependency pattern, you will need to review how each session ends and make sure each session ends by placing responsibility back on the counselee's shoulders. (Review the section on the strategy of *the punt* in chapter 7.)

Sometimes you may be doing everything right and still you sense an over attachment. When this is the case it is fair to assume that the problem stems from the counselee. At this point the best thing to do is state outright what you see happening: "X, I'm concerned that our relationship is getting unbalanced" or "Y, I see you are coming to me more and more and that concerns me."

Because confrontations are frequently taken as rejections, be sure to use "I" statements – those that begin with "I" – that are not judgmental and are easier for the person to hear. Something like, "Z, you have gotten too dependent on me and you're not taking care of yourself," would be very hard for the counselee to take and probably would be met with guilt, resistance and defensiveness, but if you say, "I am concerned that we are developing a pattern of over dependence," you will initiate a potentially productive discussion.

Correcting an over-attachment is never easy, but it is important for two reasons. First, you can't be an effective reliable-friend if you are resentful and/or overburdened. Second, letting over-attachments grow doesn't teach a healthy way for the counselee to connect with you or others and build support networks. By helping them to see the over-attachment pattern and develop new ways of interacting, you are assisting them in developing new skills for future supportive relationships.

You Don't like the Person Who Asks for Your Counsel

In the language of Transactional Analysis, "If your Child isn't in it, nothing much will happen." This means, that unless there is a positive connection on the feeling level, it will be difficult, if not impossible, to be useful to someone. It is also important for you to recognize that their intuitive request for your help indicates that from their perspective you are *their* best resource.

In cases where you don't feel a positive connection, the best you can do is be a referral resource. Point them to another counselor while remembering it is incumbent on you as a healer to respect both their intuition and your feelings. Thus you must provide them with a thoughtful referral.

Sometimes you will automatically have a person or agency in mind or you may draw a blank. When you draw a blank, tell the counselee you will need to research and find the appropriate resource and will let them know as soon as possible. This gives you time to think of another counselor or ask another for advice. Rarely, you will just not be able to come up with a direction to point them – and you must be frank with them and simply state you can't be of any help to them and they will have to seek out another resource.

There are many reasons you may not like someone – some caused by you and some will have to do with them. You might want to take time to figure out why you don't like someone with one of your personal healers. However, remember that abuse is essentially making someone or yourself not OK. For instance, even if you don't like someone, it is not OK to make them or you not OK. Just accept your feelings for what they are – basically, that you can't effectively function as a healer with that person.

Several years ago I had a person enroll in a training group for therapists. He was a close friend and classmate of someone in the group. His entrance was rather blustery and he told me he didn't have much money but still wanted to be trained. We agreed he could pay me at a later time. In the first few sessions of the group, he was obstructive and obnoxious. As I thought about his actions, I decided I would have to tell him I couldn't train him.

Surprisingly, after I got comfortable with the fact that I was going to refer him to another trainer, I began to become aware of his positive qualities. As the next training group began, it was not convenient to inform him at the beginning of the session. In that session he was neither obnoxious nor obstructive so I decided to wait a while longer before I told him of my decision.

From then on, he was a coöperative group member and I trained him through his licensing process. I was amazed. After he became licensed he moved to another community. Some four years later he showed up at my office and told me about how well his life was going. He had a thriving private practice and was doing the type of work he felt good about. I was happy for him and realized that I had come to like him. As he was ready to leave he reached into his pocket and presented me with a check for $400.

I had long since forgotten about our financial arrangement and told him so. He responded, "you may have forgotten it but I didn't." He went on to say he believed it was because I was willing to trust him to pay me when he could that our time together had been so productive. We hugged and said good-bye and I have not seen him since.

I learned a lot from that experience – most importantly that when I don't like someone and don't make them *not* OK, things change. Usually, we just go our separate ways. To quote the Gestalt prayer: "I am I and you are you. I am not in this world to meet your expectations and you are not in this world to meet mine. If we meet, it's beautiful, if we don't, it can't be helped."

You Find You Are Sexually Attracted to the Person with Whom You Are Working?

It is not unusual for persons who counsel together to experience a deep attraction for one another. In the counseling setting you are conversing on a level that is deeper than most of your conversations. Plus, you have the full focus of each other's attention with no distractions. These moments of intimate contact can easily become sexualized. This is especially true in sexually oppressed and/or sexually permissive cultures. However, even though these attractions are common, it is never – we mean NEVER – appropriate to act on these feelings.

Although there are many reason why you should not act on such impulses, none is more compelling that what Eric Berne recognized when he said, "It's a lot easier to find a good lover than it is to find a good counselor." I know of many instances where this boundary was overstepped. Yet I do not know of any cases where stepping across this boundary worked out well. Even in the situations I have known, where all the ethical prescribed actions were adhered to, still much suffering was the result of stepping across this boundary.

What do you do when you experience sexual attraction? First, it is fair to assume that when an attraction occurs with one person, it is probably happening on *some* level with the other person. Since you as the healer are directing the process, it becomes your responsibility to address the issue with your consultant. Sometimes you will want to address it with the person you are counseling after you've addressed it with *your* healer and sometimes you won't.

As a rule of thumb, always address it with your healer before you bring it into a counseling session. If your healer thinks that there is nothing wrong with acting on it, find another healer to talk with about what is happening. What you want to do is get to the heart of the issue, not get permission to do something that is potentially damaging to both of you.

The *why* of such attractions must be answered case-by-case situation. However, it's fair to assume that either one or both the parties involved is projecting something into the situation that is not in their original contract. In other words, the reason you established this relationship was to be helpful – not to find a lover – and certainly not to create even greater problems.

Having said this, we do admit it is not unusual to develop deep caring for those who help you with your problems. However, this connection is the result of sharing your mind and experience and the mutual discovery for new and better problem-solving options. Anything beyond mutual admiration and appreciation is inappropriate and potentially dangerous.

The Person You Are Counseling Is Over-Demanding

In general the over-demanding counselee is one who has not learned to deal with limits. The simple fact they are over-demanding is evidence they do not have an adequate *internal program* that helps them know when they are imposing. This is a common malady of people who reach out for counsel. When this happens, you will have to help them learn clear and appropriate limits. In such situations, it is important for you to be directive. Remember, the hallmarks of a healthy healer are that they are both *tough* and *kind* and that they know how to say *yes* and *no* to themselves and others.

The first thing to do when you feel someone is over-demanding is to make explicit what is appropriate and what is inappropriate. Next, you will need to establish an agreement that states explicitly that you will let them know whenever they are transgressing a boundary. Finally, you will need to let them know that persistent over-stepping of boundaries drives people away. Unless they learn to respect the boundaries you mutually agree upon, they may unintentionally drive you as well as others away.

The person who oversteps boundaries is almost always a person who has a dearth of friends and close associates. Helping them come to see how they are involved in their own depravation is delicate. The best way is to systematically teach them in the counseling sessions. Since, as we said, a good parent does three things: provides clear limits, provides direct nurture and provides adequate information, with the over-demanding person your parenting skills may be sorely tested.

You Can't Get a Contract for Problem Solving

Review what we've said about contracting–and the three contracting questions. Then share again with your counselee why the contract is important to your mutual success. Conclude by saying, "We won't find a clear answer to a vague question, so I am insisting that we get clear to these contracting questions before I am willing to go further into your situation."

If this doesn't work, you may need to make an interim agreement – what is called a listening contract – which says, "I will listen to your situation and ask questions for clarity but I will not suggest assignments and options until we have a contract. Is that OK with you?" After you have spent a few sessions listening, if you still cannot formulate a clearly defined, positively-stated contract, you can discuss other options for counseling – like a support group.

One person I had a difficult time establishing a contract with had been in psychoanalysis two times a week for 13 years but came to see me because she had moved away from the community where her therapist lived. She told me she originally came to therapy because she had *panic attacks* that were so severe she had to be hospitalized, but even with her analysis, the panic attacks had not subsided. Her life was controlled by her fear of the attacks and she was at the point where she couldn't enjoy her life. At age 50, she was thinking that another 13 years of this would be about all she could take. She wanted to get to the root of these attacks and have more happy times.

When she came into treatment with me she resisted the idea of a contract. "That won't work," she said, "I've always used my therapy to say whatever came to mind." I pointed out to her, albeit delicately, this approach had apparently not proven to be too successful. Then I said, "In my experience contracts work, and since you and I don't have 13 years to sort things out, let's play by my rules for six sessions. If at the end of that time you don't feel you are getting somewhere, it would probably be a good idea to find someone else to work with."

She agreed to follow my rules. At the end of six weeks

we had made significant progress and agreed to extend for another six weeks. Over the next year she made dramatic changes in her life. Her panic attacks subsided. Now she is happily retired and pursuing her hobbies with abandon. Recently, we bumped into each other in the mall. After we chatted a while I asked, "How's the panic situation." She said, "You know, it's been so long since I had a panic attack I can hardly remember what they were like."

Someone Talks Too Much

During my training I observed a group with a member who talked all the time. He would talk over anybody and bring in all sorts of extraneous information. He always had advice for everybody – little of it relevant, in my view. The therapist in charge of the group was very directive – to the point of being almost brutal, but she couldn't contain him and finally kicked him out of the group.

As luck would have it, he called me for an appointment some years later. He had recently married and his new wife was about to leave him. I reluctantly agreed to see them. Not surprisingly he came in with a barrage of words. I reminded him of his time with his previous therapist.

"If we are going to work together," I said, "I will have to have some control over who talks and how much they talk." He fell silent and appeared to be a little hurt.

I turned to his new wife, "Harry tells me you are about to leave, is that true."

"Yes," she said.

"What is the problem?"

"He talks all the time. I mean *all* the time. Even while we are making love he is talking. I can't stand it."

He started to interrupt and I "shsst" him. We sat in quiet for a while. Several more times he started to talk and I "shsst" him.

Finally, I turned to him and asked how it felt while we were quiet.

"Terrible," he said.

"Are you willing to deal with that *terrible* feeling?" I asked.

"Yes," he said.

We made a contract to deal with his feelings and he came into private treatment where he dealt with his responses. As he resolved his own issues, the marriage improved. In the final analysis, Harry and Jill stayed married and as far as I know are living together in harmony.

The point is, if you are dealing with someone who talks too much, you will need to help him discover and explore what his talking is masking. This is a task for psychotherapy and you will be best off to make a good referral.

Someone Won't Talk

Seldom will someone come to you for counsel and not talk. However, occasionally such is the case. Here are three case scenarios:

CASE #1:

Lilly came into treatment sat down and didn't say a word. She had called for an appointment saying that Jim, one of my clients, had suggested she come to counseling. I asked several questions and she gave me terse brief answers. Finally, she said, "I just don't want to talk."

"Well," I said, "I'm willing to just sit with you for a while, if that is what you want." I based this on my knowledge that respecting and following the wants of someone builds trust. We sat for about 30 minutes and then I asked if she was ready to talk.

"No" she said, shyly.

"Would it be OK with you if I just told you what I was thinking as we set together?"

"Yes," she responded, in a painfully shy manner.

Again, we took a small step towards a relationship built on trust as she was willing to stay in what was, at the present, an awkward and distressing situation for her. For the rest of the session I reported on my random thoughts as they occurred. When time was up she made another appointment. For several weeks we followed that same protocol and slowly she began to talk more and more. Soon we were having normal sessions and discussing how her shyness kept her from enjoying her life.

From working with Lilly, I learned that accepting someone where they were and just being with them was an essential first step. By sitting quietly with her and respecting her desires, I tuned into my intuition. As I reported on the thoughts going on in my head and how I was feeling, it was not surprising that some of my thoughts paralleled her process and she discovered we had things to talk about.

She, like all of us, needed to know that there was

someone who would listen to her – even her silence. Once she felt respected and listened to, she began to be free to express her confusion and questions.

CASE #2:

Roger was a successful clergyperson. He was much in demand as a speaker and leader of youth. He called and asked to see me because one of his main mentors had died and he couldn't seem to get over it. On the phone he said he wasn't able to keep his appointments and felt like a failure as a Christian and he needed to talk to someone. He arrived punctually at the appointed time and greeted me in his warm friendly/ministerial way and sat down.

"How are things going?" I queried.

He looked at me, opened his mouth and nothing came out. He made a little hand motion and tried again to speak. His eyes welled with tears and he turned his head away. For the next ten minutes he tried to speak and I sat quietly. Finally, he said , "I'm a failure," and began to cry.

Roger couldn't speak because he was overloaded with feelings. His thoughts were jumbled and confused. He had to purge the feelings and clarify his thinking before he could get on with his life. In the long run he had to reclaim his humanity and give up some false notions of what a "minister" was.

In physics there is a law: "Energy can be transformed, it cannot be made to disappear." This law applies to psychology as well. In Roger's case, the energy of his grief and his concept of himself as a minister were blocking his full expression of his feelings. This pent-up energy was overwhelming him and keeping him from functioning. He needed a safe place to feel and express his grief. Until he found it, his feelings were overwhelming him.

CASE # 3:

Frequently you will be confronted with someone who won't talk. This is most common when you counsel couples. One or the other doesn't talk – and most likely this will be the male who won't talk. But the same principles apply when a female won't talk.

Ted and Alice made an appointment to discuss their relationship. As soon as they sat down Ted said: "This is her idea, I don't have anything to talk about." Alice went into a well-rehearsed tirade that covered most of the shortcomings anyone could possibly have.

"Well, you see why I won't talk," Ted said.

"I get a general idea, but I would like for you to tell me."

"If I say anything, it will make things worse – so I'm not saying anything more."

At that point I took charge and said, "If you are going to work with me to straighten out this relationship, I want to spend the first few sessions focusing on what you like about each other, what brought you together in the first place and what is good about the relationship in the present. I think you can understand the reason for my requirements."

They agreed to my demands and both showed relief; then we proceeded. Throughout the sessions I focused on getting them to talk about what they liked about each other. As they began to hear one another, they reëstablished the secure, caring base of their relationship. Once this was in place, they were free to deal with the petty, stylistic irritations that were threatening their relationship.

As far as I know, they are still together after about six months of working on their relationship. The point is people like Ted refuse to talk when they can't find any way to make things better. Here it is the healer's responsibility to provide the way.

You Dread Meetings with the Person

Anytime you find you are apprehensive about meeting with a counselee, it's time to reassess. First you need to think back and ascertain when these feelings began. Perhaps it was because your own life got busy or complicated – which means it may be time to restate your own limits. Sometimes though, when everything seems to be going fine, you will come upon a topic in your conversations, as a reliable-friend, that makes you uncomfortable. Instead of recognizing this right away, you may just begin to dread talking with that person.

At this point it's time to talk with your healer. You will need to discuss the feelings and issues that have been brought up and whether or not you want to continue working with this person. It is best to make a referral to someone else whenever you can't willingly respond to someone's need. No one likes to be merely tolerated.

A long-time friend, Tracy, has come to me many times to discuss her obsessive problems. When we talked, I began finding I was slipping into thinking about my problems along the same line (parallel process) and began obsessing myself. I needed to decide whether I wanted to work on my own stuff–my obsessions–needed to stop working with Tracy. After discussing this with my own healer and receiving counsel, I told Tracy of my predicament of dealing with many of the same issues and finding it tough to stay on track when we were talking. We decided I was not her best resource on that topic. She still counts me a reliable friend and we at times even discuss her obsessions–but being more aware, I am now able to keep from slipping into this parallel process.

You Realize an Issue Is More Serious than You Originally Thought

When you find you are in over your head and feel unqualified to handle the situation, remember you are a reliable-friend, not a *savior.* The person came to you because they felt you were their best resource. Be straight with them and talk to them about going to see a professional, offer some recommendations, check in with them to see how their doing. Offer to help them find the right kind of help. Let them know that you care. If need be, arrange to go with them to a counselor.

In Conclusion

As you begin to see yourself as a reliable-friend and realize you have the skills to respond as a healer, many opportunities to practice these new skills will come your way. Remember, it is always okay to refer the person to someone who can help. The important thing is to recognize and operate within your limits. This isn't copping out; it's being a *good* and *reliable-friend*.

Each of us has within us the gift of healing others, as well as the need to be healed by others. This book is simply meant to be a guide on the journey.

9

In Summary

A Personal Conclusion from Denton

My first grandchild was born as we were writing this book. As I observed his mother and father caring for their first-born, I was aware afresh of the power of interdependent relationships. My son and daughter-in-law are giving protection, nourishment and warmth, and my new grandson, in his own natural way, is giving joy, pride and fulfillment.

Watching this threesome, I am inspired and it warms my heart, I am keenly aware that the conditions they create for him are not only his birthright, but everyone's birthright. Further, I know that my grandson's needs for protection, warmth and nourishment will not end when he reaches some magical age of maturity. He, like you and I, will need others to turn to throughout his life. Even on his deathbed, he will need others to supply his basic human need for healthy inter-dependence.

At sometime in the future, you may be the person my grandson turns to. If you have prepared yourself to meet his need, he will be better able to solve his dilemma and be the person he is capable of being. This awesome responsibility of being the one who helps him out in his time of trouble I am passing on to you. Let me thank you in advance for meeting his need.

A Personal Word from Caddy

Finding and releasing the healer within myself has been a joyful, learning experience. I know within my heart, that the quality of relationships shapes the quality of our lives. As I release the healer within, my life is enhanced; however, allowing another to act as my healer has been harder for me.

For many of us it is difficult to accept healing or any gift from others. Perhaps this comes from a need to be independent or an unwillingness to accept that we NEED *anything outside ourselves. Many of us feel it is a sign of weakness to* NEED *something from someone. In no other part of my life has this been more important than with the people I love the most, my husband Adrian and son Antaeus.*

Adrian and I had been in a relationship for only a few months when my Aunt Jerry died after a long terminal illness. At the memorial service Adrian became very emotional, which I hadn't expected. Afterwards he shared with me that his uncle had died before we had met. Many times we fail to remember we are healers within our own family. I see that, in fact, this is my truest purpose.

Denton L. Roberts, M.Div., an ordained minister and a marriage family therapist, is a certified Clinical Teaching and Supervising Transactional Analyst who has spent his career helping "common people" live in peaceful healing relationships. Other books of his include *Able and Equal (A Gentler Path to Peace); Lumps and Bumps (A Children's Book for Parents and a Parents' Book for Children)*; and *Find Purpose–Find Power (Sing the Song in Your Heart)*. During his 35-year career he has focused on building therapeutic relationships and communities training people workers in the U.S., Europe and Russia.

Caddy Roberts-Williams, a natural therapist who works with at-risk children, youth and parents, comes with experience as a counselor and advocate in a variety of settings. She is a La Leche League leader, the founder of More-Mentoring, a community-wide program for at-risk youth, and a group skills leader in court-appointed drug diversion programs. She uses her natural skill and sensitivity to assist people in living in supportive healing relationships.

Additional copies of this book
may be obtained from your bookstore
or by contacting

Hope Publishing House
P.O. Box 60008
Pasadena, CA 91116
(626) 792-6123 / (800) 326-2671
Fax (626) 792-2121

E-mail: hopepub@loop.com
Visit our Web site: http://www.hope-pub.com